Euphemia Vale Blake

The Universal Name

100 Songs to Mary

Euphemia Vale Blake

The Universal Name
100 Songs to Mary

ISBN/EAN: 9783337006907

Printed in Europe, USA, Canada, Australia, Japan

Cover: Foto ©Thomas Meinert / pixelio.de

More available books at **www.hansebooks.com**

THE UNIVERSAL NAME

OR

ONE HUNDRED SONGS TO MARY

SELECTED AND ARRANGED

BY

MRS. E. VALE BLAKE

BUFFALO
CHARLES WELLS MOULTON
1894

TO

MISS MARY C. LOWELL

OF BROOKLYN, N. Y.,

THESE VERSES ARE AFFECTIONATELY

INSCRIBED BY THE

AUTHOR AND COMPILER.

PREFACE.

THERE are over fifty different forms of the name of Mary in use in Europe; many of these are derived from the Hebrew word Miriam, which was the real name, of she whom we call Mary, the mother of Jesus. The Greeks and Latins translated it Maria, the French Marie; the English alone translated it Mary. The Slavonic races have such derivatives as Marika. In western Europe we have the variations of Marion, Marietta, &c.; the returning Crusaders brought the name to Spain, France and Great Britain. It found a cordial reception, and has been for centuries the most popular name in Christendom, including the United States. Among the Latin races it is often bestowed on male children.

There have been more poems written, addressed to Mary, than any other name known to literature. Of the few here collected we have given the name of the author whenever that was known, but very many of the songs, poems and ballads have been long floating round the world without any known parentage; any deficiency in this respect we should be happy to supply in a future edition if the authorship can be authenticated.

E. V. B.

BROOKLYN, N. Y.
1894.

∴ CONTENTS ∴

CONTENTS.

CONTENTS.

CONTENTS.

THE UNIVERSAL NAME.

In the Christian World, Mary, the Garland Wears.—CHARLES LAMB.

"I have a passion for the name of Mary."—LORD BYRON.

MARY is sounding in our ears,
  From palace and from cot;
What place, of high or low degree
  Where this loved name is not?

We read it oft in sacred writ,
  This, poets most admire;
We see it oft on History's page,
  No name exalted higher.

And Mary's name we love it still,
  In palace or in cot;
It makes our very heart strings thrill,
  Who is there loves it not?

L'INCONNUE.

IS thy name Mary maiden fair?
  Such should methinks its music be;
The sweetest name that mortals bear
  Were best befitting thee;
And she to whom it once was given,
Was half of earth and half of heaven.

I hear thy voice, I see thy smile,
  I look upon thy folded hair;
Ah! while we dream not they beguile,
  Our hearts are in the snare;
And she who claims a wild bird's wing,
Must start not if her captive sing.

So lady, take the leaf that falls,
  To all but thee unseen, unknown;
When evening shades thy silent walls,
  Then read it all alone;
In stillness read, in darkness seal,
Forget, condemn, but not reveal.

                    OLIVER WENDELL HOLMES.

MARY.

WHAT though the name is old and oft repeated,
    What though a thousand beings bear it now,
And true hearts oft the gentle word have greeted—
    What though 'tis hallowed by a poet's vow?
We ever love the rose, and yet its blooming
    Is a familiar rapture to the eye:
And yon bright star we hail, although its looming
    Age after age has lit the northern sky.

As starry beam o'er troubled billows stealing,
    As garden odors to the desert blown,
In bosoms faint a gladsome hope revealing,
    Like patriot music or affection's tone:
Thus, thus, for aye, the name of Mary spoken
    By lips or text, with magic-like control.
The course of present thought has quickly broken,
    And stirred the fountains of my inmost soul.

The sweetest tales of human weal and sorrow,
    The fairest trophies of the limner's fame,
To my fond fancy, Mary, seem to borrow,
    Celestial halos from thy gentle name:
The Grecian artist gleaned from many faces,
    And in a perfect whole the parts combined,
So have I counted o'er dear woman's graces,
    To form the Mary of my ardent mind.

And marvel not I thus call my ideal—
   We inly paint as we would have things be:
The fanciful springs ever from the real,
   As Aphrodite rose from out the sea.
Who smiled upon me kindly, day by day
   In a far land, where I was sad and lone?
Whose presence now is my delight alway?
   Both angels must the same blessed title own.

What spirits round my weary way are flying,
   What fortunes on my future life await?
Like the mysterious hymns the winds are sighing,
   Are all unknown—in trust I bide my fate:
But if one blessing I might crave from Heaven,
   'Twould be that Mary should my being cheer,
Hang o'er me when the chord of life is riven,
   Be my dear household word, and my last accent hear.
               HENRY THEODORE TUCKERMAN.

MY MARY.

WHEN Mary met my wondering eyes
   ⌐She was a little elf,
So fair, so canny and so wise
   I said within myself—
" O mystery of mysteries
   Thou tiny little creature,
Thou com'st express from Paradise
   To be thy Father's teacher."

And then she grew, until I knew
   She still was something more
Than a mere flower, from heavenly bower,
   Come floating down the air.
Her face was fair, her soul was rare,
   And hidden powers revealed,
And I began to pray and scan
   For virtues still concealed.
So with the years, my hopes and fears
   Compelled me oft to cry—
"O wondrous girl, I'm but a churl
   To have the care of thee."

But lo! before I learned the lore
   From whence my Mary grew,
She taught it me, upon my knee
   And on my bosom too.
Teacher at once, and scholar too—
   Guide, guider, watcher, ward,
My pride, my peace, my strength, my joy,
   My angel from the Lord.
            J. P. L.   *In Christian Register.*

AVE MARIA—EL VAQUERO.

"AVE MARIA," a herder said,
   One eve in sight of Santa Fé;
Where ground and blanket were his bed,
   And all around his cattle lay.

"Ave Maria full of grace—"
　How strangely solemn were the words,
In such a wild and dreary place,
　Beneath the stars, among the herds.

" Santa Maria, Mother of God:"
　Angel like breezes came to take
The words thus spoken, from the sod,
　To yonder sky while yet he spake.

" Pray for us sinners now," said he,
　With earnest hope to be forgiven:
While distant hills all seemed to be
　Steps leading from the plains to Heaven.

" Pray for us in the hour of death,"
　And softly still the murmuring came,
Until at last the lisping breath—
　Ceased—with the sweet and holy name.

"Ave Maria," no more he said
　That eve, in sight of Santa Fé;
When morning came, a herder dead
　Was found there—where his cattle lay.

J. C. BURNET.

MARY.

"THE prettiest, tiniest little head
    That ever sat on an ivory neck,
So smooth and so rounded without a fleck,
That jewels were wasted such throat to deck,
In its muslin frill, like pearl in its bed;
With a flood of soft rippling nut-brown hair
Reflecting in gold the kiss of the air;

Ears small and so perfect—that by him seen,
Praxiteles' models they might have been,
To complete his statue of Beauty's queen;
And eyes, like turquois and sapphire mingled;
A voice as when silvery bells are tingled:
And withal so saucy! there's not a grace
But finds a fit home in that charming face.
              Harper's Magazine, January, 1882.

OUT TO OLD AUNT MARY'S.

WASN'T it pleasant, O! brother mine,
    In those old days of the lost sunshine
Of youth—when the Saturday's chores were through,
And the Sunday's wood in the kitchen too,
And we went visiting, I and you
      Out to old Aunt Mary's?

It all comes back so clear to-day!
Though I am as bald as you are gray—
Out by the barn-lot and down the lane
We patter along in the dust again,
As light as the tips of the drops of the rain
              Out to old Aunt Mary's!

We cross the pasture, and through the wood
Where the old gray snag of the poplar stood,
Where the hammering redheads hopped away,
And the buzzard raised in the open sky
And lolled and circled as we went by
              Out to old Aunt Mary's!

And then in the dust of the road again,
And the teams we met and the countrymen,
And the long highway with the sunshine spread
As thick as butter on country bread,
And our cares behind and our hearts ahead,
              Out to old Aunt Mary's!

I see her now in the open door,
Where the little gourds grew up the sides and on
The clapboard roof.   And her face—oh me!
Wasn't it good for a boy to see?
And wasn't it good for the boy to be
              Out to old Aunt Mary's?

And oh! my brother, so far away,
This is to tell you she waits to-day

To welcome us, Aunt Mary fell
Asleep this morning, whispering, "Tell
The boys to come!" And all is well
Out to old Aunt Mary's.

JAMES WHITCOMB RILEY.

HOW MARY GREW.

(ADDRESSED TO MISS MARY GREW).

WITH wisdom far beyond her years,
  And graver than her wondering peers,
So strong, so mild, combining still,
The tender heart and queenly will,
  To conscience and to duty true
  So up from childhood, Mary Grew!

Then in her gracious womanhood,
She gave her days to doing good,
She dared the scornful laugh of men,
The hounding mob, the slanderer's pen,
  So did the work she found to do,
  A christian heroine, Mary Grew!

The freed slave thanks her; blessing comes
To her, from woman's weary homes;
The wronged and erring find in her
The censor mild, and comforter.
  The world were safe, if but a few
  Could grow in grace as Mary Grew.

So New Year's Eve, I sit and say,
By this low wood fire, ashen grey;
Just wishing as the night shuts down,
That I could hear in Boston town,
  In pleasant Chestnut Avenue
  From her own lips, how Mary Grew!

And hear her graceful hostess tell,
The silver-voicéd oracle—
Who lately through her parlors spoke
As through Dodona's sacred oak;
A wiser truth than any told
By Sappho's lips of ruddy gold—
  The way to make the world anew
  Is just to grow—as Mary Grew!
              JOHN GREENLEAF WHITTIER.

THOUGHTS OF MARY ON THE POTOMAC.

ALL quiet along the Potomac they say—
  Except now and then a stray picket
Is shot, as he walks on his beat to and fro
  By a rifleman hid in the thicket.
'Tis nothing; a private or two now and then
  Will not count in the news of the battle;
Not an officer lost, only one of the men
  Moaning out, all alone, the death rattle.

All quiet along the Potomac to-night,
　Where the soldiers lie peacefully dreaming
Their tents in the rays of the clear autumn moon,·
　Or the light of the watch-fires are gleaming.
A tremulous sigh, as the gentle night wind
　Through the forest leaves gently is creeping,
While stars up above, with their glittering eyes
　Keep guard,—for the army is sleeping.

There's only the sound of the lone sentry's tread,
　As he tramps from the rock to the fountain,
And thinks of the two in the lone trundle bed,
　Far away in the cot, on the mountain.
His musket falls slack, his face dark and grim,
　Glows gentle with memories tender,
As he mutters a prayer for the children asleep;
　For their mother—may heaven defend her!

The moon seems to shine just as brightly as then
　That night when the love yet unspoken,
Leapt up to his lips, when low, murmured vows
　Were pledged to be ever unbroken;
Then drawing his sleeve roughly over his eyes
　He dashes off tears that are welling,
And gathers his gun closer up to his side
　As if to keep down the heart swelling.

He passes the fountain, the blasted pine tree,
　The footstep is lagging and weary,
Yet onward he goes through the broad belt of light
　T'ward the shade of the forest so dreary.

Hark! was it the night-wind that rustled the leaves,
  Was it moonlight so wondrously flashing?
It looked like a rifle—"Ah! Mary, good-bye,"
  And the life-blood is ebbing and plashing.

All quiet along the Potomac to-night,
  No sound, save the rush of the river;
While soft falls the dew on the face of the dead
  The picket's off duty forever.
Hark! was it the night-wind that rustled the leaves,
  Was it moonlight so wondrously plashing?
It looked like a rifle—"Ah! Mary, good-bye,"
  And the life-blood is ebbing and flashing.
                    MRS. ETHEL LYNN BEERS.

AN AMERICAN "AVE MARIA."

"AVE MARIA," 'tis the evening hymn,
    Of many pilgrims on the land and sea;
  Soon as the day withdraws, and two or three
Faint stars are burning, all whose eyes are dim
With tears or watching, all of weary limb,
  Or troubled spirit, yield the bended knee,
  And find, O! Virgin, life's repose in thee.
I too, at nightfall, when the new born rim
  Of the young moon is first beheld above,
    Tune my fond thoughts to their devoutest key,

And from all bondage—save remembrance, free,
Glad of my liberty as Noah's dove,
  Seek the Madona most adored by me,
And say my "Ave Maria's" to my love.
                          THOMAS WILLIAM PARSONS.

MARY PRESCOTT.

(A REMINISENCE).

IF I had thought so soon she would have died,
  He said, I had been tenderer in my speech,
I had a moment lingered at her side,
  And held her, ere she passed beyond my reach;
If I had thought so soon she would have died.

That day she looked up with her startled eyes,
  Like some hurt creature, where the woods are deep:
With kisses I had stilled those breaking sighs,
  With kisses closed those eyelids into sleep,
That day she looked up with her startled eyes,

Oh! had I known she would have died so soon,
  Love had not wasted on a barren land,
Love, like those rivers under torrid noon
  Lost on the desert, poured out on the sand—
Oh! had I known she would have died so soon.
                          HARRIET PRESCOTT SPOFFORD.

TO LITTLE MARY L——.

O DARLING Mary L——.
We love you more than well
For your charming winsome ways
Are so bonnie!
Though ye'r na' from "auld Scotland
Wi' their brawest ye can stan'
Wi' ye'r ee o' blue sae kind, and
Smile so sunny!

O darling Mary L——.
May ye outshine them a'
In good and gentle ways
Sweet and bonnie!
May ye set no store on beauty
And forever rule yoursel'
By the grace of Love and Duty
Blessings on ye, Mary L——.
1884.   E. V. B.

WEE MARIAN B——.

MARIAN'S eyes are greyish blue,
            Greyish blue;
But they straightway look you through
            Look you through.
Her voice is bright and clear,
As it falls upon the ear—
            Ringing true.

Sweet Marian's but a bud yet,
            A bud yet;
Wait until she grows,
            Till she grows,
Then we'll have the sweetness
Then we'll see the beauty of the rose
            The perfect rose!
1885.   E. V. B.

TO MISS MARY C——.

(ON HER RETURN TO BERMUDA).

CHILD of the sea, why did'st thou come
        Far from thy native Isle
To shine a moment in our homes
And all our hearts beguile.

We've seen thee in thy days of joy,
  We've mourned with thee in sorrow;
And prayed for thee, that every day
  Might bring a bright to-morrow.

But now, our " Vision of Delight "
  Is passing from our view,
But space can not efface our love
  Our hearts will sail with you.

E. V. B.

I DINNA FIND MY MARY.

MY Mary! O my Mary!
  The simmer skies are blue;
The dawning brings the dazzle,
  The gloamin' brings the dew—
The mirk o' nicht the glory
  O' the moon, and kindles too
The stars that shift about the lift,
  But nae thing brings me you!

Where is it, O, my Mary,
  Ye are biding a' the while?
I ha' wended by your window—
  I ha' waited at the stile:
And up and down the river
  I ha' rowed for mony a mile,
Yet never found it, drift or drowned,
  Your long belated smile.

Is it forgot, my Mary,
  How glad we used to be ?
The simmer time, when bonnie
  Bloomed the auld trysting tree—
How there I carved a name for you,
  And you a name for me;
And the twilight kenned it only,
  When we kissed sae tenderly.

Speak aince to me, my Mary—
  But whisper in my ear,
As light as ony sleeper's breath,
  And a' my soul will hear;
My heart shall stop its beating,
  And the soughing atmosphere
Be hushed, the while I leaning smile
  And listen to you, dear.

My Mary! O my Mary!
  The blossoms bring the bees,
The sunshine brings the blossoms
  And the leaves upon the trees.
The simmer brings the sunshine,
  And the fragrance of the breeze,
But O, without you, Mary,
  I care nae thing for these!

We were sae happy, Mary!
  O think how aince we said—
Wad ane o' us gang fickle,
  Or ane o' us were dead—

To feel anither's kisses
  We wad feign the auld instead,
And ken the ither's footsteps
  In the grass aboon the head.

My Mary! O, my Mary!
  Are ye sister o' the air?
That ye vanish aye before me
  As I follow everywhere.
Or is it that ye're only
  But a mortal wan wi' care?
Sin' I search the kirkyard over
  And dinna find you there!
                JAMES WHITCOMB RILEY.

MY MARY.

(OLD SONG.)

KIND, kind, gentle is she,
    Kind is my Mary;
The sweetest blossom on the tree
  Can not compare with Mary!

So when I see some bonnie lass,
  I step aside and let her pass,
For O! for O! she's not the lass,
  For O! she's not my Mary!

Kind, kind, gentle is she,
    Kind is my Mary;
The sweetest blossom on the tree
    Can not compare with Mary!

MY SWEET AND DELICATE MARIE.

MY sweet and delicate *Marie*,
    I used to call you *Mary!*
By either name you were to me
    A most undoubted fairy;
But as you grew in years and stature,
You changed alike in name and nature.

I used to think your eyes of blue,
    Your almost perfect features,
Were beauty's models, and that you
    The rarest of earth's creatures,
Eclipsed in every situation
The best effects of decoration.

But now your gentle tone is changed
    To me it is a war-song—
And we so far apart have ranged
    That we might play " Divorcons,"
In fact we get along as badly
As if I once had loved you madly.

Alone you pick your airy way
  Among your " Rose de Barry,"
Faience, Satsuma, Cloisonné,
  And vow you ne'er will marry,
While I about the bookstores wander
And over old editions ponder.

My sweet and delicate Marie
  Whom I admired as Mary,
Love can not stay with such as we
  Whose tastes so widely vary.
You say that my pursuits are mussy
And I am sure that yours are fussy.

EDWARD WILLETT.

THE EMPIRE OF THE MIND, MARY.

NO—not the eye of tender blue,
  Though Mary, 'twere the tint of thine;
Or breathing lip of glowing hue,
  Might bid the opening bud repine
      Had long enthralled my mind, Mary.

Nor tint with tint, alternate aiding,
  That o'er the dimpled tablet flow,
The vermeil to the lily fading!
  Nor ringlet bright, with orient glow,
      In many a tendril twined, Mary.

The breathing tint, the beamy ray
The lineal harmony divine,
That o'er the form of beauty play,
Might warm a colder heart than mine,
But not forever bind, Mary.

But when to radiant form and feature
Internal worth and feeling join;
With temper mild and gay good nature,
Aróund the willing heart they twine
The Empire of the mind, Mary.

PRETTY MARY, O!

NO more with tears I count the years,
When sorrow wooed me long ago:
Though hearts must bleed when they have need,
And friend may wound you worse than foe.
Smiles come at last, when grief goes past;
But oh! our thoughts did vary so;
When I sat back, with head bowed down,
And you stood up before the town,
A-marrying pretty Mary, O!

O! fairest maid, through sun and shade
And storm and darkness brooding so;
She was my star, that smiled afar,
The only light I cared to know.

You soared on high and from the sky
  My pretty star bore swiftly, Joe:
And then to say, "God bless you both,"
It tore me like a cruel oath,
  When you had wed my Mary, O!

O! time has wings that bring sweet things,
  To hide the wounds that rend us so;
A winsome touch, that thrills me much
  Is now upon my shoulder, Joe!
And gentle eyes, whose light 1 prize
  More than all dreams I used to know,
Look into mine, and we renew
And send the thankful love of two,
  To Joe and pretty Mary, O!

                    BENJAMIN S. PARKER.

A' FOR MARY.

I KEN a wud whaur the breezes sing
  Tae nicht frae mornin' early,
Whaur ilka bird on flutt'rin' wing,
  Joins in the chorus rarely;
An' aye my fancy forms the sang—
  Hooe'er its notes may vary,
Tae this, the chief a' themes amang,
  "The warl' an a' for Mary."

I ken a water, dancin' licht
  At simmer morn an' gloamin',
Adoon the rocks like siller bricht,
  An, then o'er meadows roamin'.
It has a liltin', joyous note,
  Saft as sang o' fairy
And this is aye the burden o't,
  "The warl' an a' for Mary."

I ken a heart, nae sayin' whaur,
  That lo'es this wordless tunin'
That hears nae soon' frae stream or scaur,
  But love is aye communin';
It has nae wish itsel' tae free
  Frae fancy's wild vagary,
An' weel I ken that heart wud gie
  "The warl' an a' for Mary."

WILLIAM LYLE.

MARION MOORE.

GONE art thou, Marion, Marion Moore!
  Gone like the bird in the autumn that singeth,
Gone like the flower by the wayside that springeth,
Gone like the leaf of the ivy that clingeth
Round the lone rock on a storm beaten shore.

Dear wert thou, Marion, Marion Moore!
  Dear as the tide in my broken heart throbbing,
  Dear as the soul o'er thy memory sobbing,
  Sorrow my life of its roses is robbing
Wasting is all the glad beauty of yore.

I will remember thee, Marion Moore!
  I shall remember, alas, to regret thee,
  I will regret when all others forget thee
  Deep in my breast will the hour that I met thee,
Linger and burn till Life's fever is o'er.

Gone art thou, Marion, Marion Moore!
  Gone like the breeze o'er the billow that bloweth;
  Gone like the rill to the ocean that floweth;
  Gone as the day, from the grey mountain goeth,
Darkness behind thee, but glory before.

Peace to thee, Marion, Marion Moore!
  Peace which the queens of the earth can not borrow;
  Peace from a kingdom that crowned thee with sorrow,
  O! to be happy with thee, on the morrow,
Who would not fly from this desolate shore?

                    JAMES GAYLORD CLARK.

MARY, LIST! AWAKE!

MARY, dear Mary, list! awake!
    And now like the moon thy slumbers break.
There is not a taper, and scarcely a sound
To be seen, or be heard in the cottages round;
The watch-dog is silent, thy father sleeps,
But love, like the breeze, to thy window creeps:
    The moonlight seems listening all over the land,
        To the whispers of angels like thee;
    O! lift but a moment the sash with thine hand,
        And kiss but that hand to me.
            My love Mary,
        Kiss but that hand to me!

Gently awake, and gently rise,
Oh! for a kiss to unclose thine eyes!
The vapors of sleep shall fly softly the while,
As the breath on thy mirror breaks at thy smile,
And then I would whisper thee, never to fear,
For Heaven is all round thee when true love is near.
    Just under the woodbine, dear Mary I stand,
        Still looking and list'ning for thee;
    O! lift but a moment the sash with thine hand
        And kiss but that hand to me,
            My love Mary,
        And kiss but that hand to me!

Hark! do I hear thee?—Yes! 'tis thou,
And there is thy hand—I see thee now;
Thou look'st like a rose in a crystal stream,
For thy face, love, is bathed in the moonlight gleam;
And oh! could my kisses like stream-circles rise,
To dip in thy dimples, and spread round thine eyes.
  How sweet to be lost in a night such as this,
   In the arms of an angel like thee.
  Nay, stay but a moment—one moment of bliss,
   And smile but forgiveness to me!
    My love, Mary,
   Smile but forgiveness to me!

Nobody, sweet, can hear our sighs,
Thy voice, just comes on the soft air and dies;
Dost thou gaze on the moon, as I've gazed as I rove?
Till I thought it had breathed Heaven's blessings on love,
Till I've stretched out my arms, and my tears have begun,
And Nature and Heaven and Thou seemed but One.
  Fare thee well, sweetest Mary, the moon's in the west,
   And the leaves shine with tear-drops like thee;
  So draw in thy charms, and betake thee to rest,
   O! thou dearer than life to me.
    My love, Mary,
   Thou dearer than life to me!

THE MARIGOLDE.

The following is one of the quaintest poems of its era: it is a panegyric upon QUEEN MARY TUDOR. The original is preserved in the archives of the library of the Society of Antiquaries at Somerset House. It is very lengthy and we can give but a few excerpts. The poet after describing the virtues of other flowers, proceeds thus:—

THIS marigolde floure, mark it well,
    With Sonne doth open and also shut:
Which (in a meaning) to us doth tell,
    To Christ, God's Sonne, our wills to put;
And by his worde to set our futte,
    Stifly to stand as champions bolde:
For the truth, nor to stagger nor stutter:
    For which I praise the marigolde.

To *Marie* our Queen, that floure so sweet,
    This marigolde I doe apply,
For that the name doth serve to meete,
    And propertee in each partie:
To her enduring patiently
    The storms of such as list to scolde
At her dooyings, without cause why;
    Loth to see spring this marigolde.

She may be called Marigolde well,
    Of Marie's (chief) Christe's mother deere,
That as in heaven shee doth excell,
    And Gold on earth it hath no peare:

So certainly Shee shineth cleere.
   In grace and honor double folde;
The like was never earst seen heere;
   Such is this floure—the marigolde.

*   *   *   *   *   *

If she (in faith) had erred a-misse
   Which God most sure doth understand,
Would he have done as provèd is,
   Her enemies so to bring to hande?
No, be ye sure; I make a bande,
   For servying him, he needs so wold
Make her to reign over England;
   So loveth hee this Marigolde.

Her conversation note who list,
   It is more heavenly than terraine,
For which God doth her acts assist;
   All meekness doth in her remaine;
All is her care, how to ordainne,
   To have God's glory here extolde;
Of poor and rich she is most fayne;
   Christ save therefore this Marygolde.

Sith, so it is, God loveth her,
   And she his grace as doth appear:
Ye may be bolde as to referre,
   All doubtfullness, to her most cleare,
That as her owne, in like manneare,
   She with your welthes, both young and olde;
Obey her then, as your Queen deare,
   And say, " Christe save this Marigolde."

TO MARY THE BLESSÈD MOTHER.

(FROM AN OLD ENGLISH PASSION PLAY, OF DATE 1264).

"HAIL, O hail, all peerless Maiden!
　　Thine enclasping arm is laden,
With a child whose ages number
　　God's eternity.
Let us worship him in slumber
　　On his mother's knee.

Mary by thy mediation
Grant our sinful souls salvation!
Though as wheat the devil sift us,
　　Hold us in thy sight,
That thy Son at last may lift us
　　To his blessèd light!"

TO QUEEN MARY STUART.

O! BONNIE Mary Stuart,
　　In Lochleven keep:
There's muckle dool before ye,
Life's road is rough an' steep.

The nicht-bird croaks fra' eerie,
  On the auld castle wa'
An' aye it sings sae weirdly—
  Oh, dinna' gang awa'—
      " Dinna leave the braw Scotch hills,
        Whaur hearts are gude an' true,
      And dinna cross the border,
        Or sair the day ye'll rue."

I had a wakefu' dream yestreen,
  Of treason, bluidy red—
I saw a ghastly marchin'
  Gae slowly past my bed;
I saw an axe like siller
  A dark cheil' bore alang,
An' roon' him flew the corbie
  Wi' his uncanny sang—
      " Had ye no' left the mountains,
        Whaur hearts are guid an' true,
      Had ye no' crossed the border
        Ye wadna' had tae rue."

She crossed the Scottish border,
  She met her Judas frien';
Waes me for Mary Stuart,
  Our bonny martyr Queen,
Weary fa' ye Jezebel,
  There's bluid upon yer name,
Time ne'er will wipe the stainin'
  Fra' yer unqueenly fame.

She pined for mony winters,
　　Then paid a debt, no due.
Sae fell our Scottish Mary—
　　The corbie's sang cam' true.

WILLIAM LYLE.

QUEEN MARY AT FOTHERINGAY.

AH, wearily and woe is me!
　　Ah, wearily the time drifts on;
Unrestful, of a verity,
　　The life whose love of life is gone,
No heartsome sports the hours engross,
　　A nerveless round consumes the day,
To broider hems, or gaze across
　　The dreary flats of Fotheringay.

I hear, through distant forest glades
　　The falconer ride by the banks of Nenne,
'Mid tuneful madrigals of maids
　　And deep toned notes of Englishmen.
I'd rather be the dove they kill,
　　Sating their talons with my blood,
Than being a falcon at their will
　　Return obedient to the hood.

What love, what royal clemency,
　　O, sister Queen, Elizabeth,
Yon gloomy bastions testify,
　　This captive woman witnesseth!

My realm four roods of prison ground,
  Four faithful leiges left alone,
My Maries four, that hover round
  Their Mary's shadow of a throne.

O! Mary mother, maid divine,
  That sittest in the height serene,
A sorry plight on earth was mine
  To be a woman and a Queen!
Soon may these mortal prison bars,
  Before my white winged soul be riven
Soon may it soar above the stars
  And win the bonnie hills of Heaven.

MAG. ART.

QUEEN MARY'S ESCAPE FROM LOCHLEVEN CASTLE.

(AIR: HIGHLAND BOAT).

PUT off, put off, and row with speed!
    For now's the time and the hour of need!
To oars, to oars, and trim the bark,
Nor Scotland's Queen be a warder's mark;
Yon light that plays round the castle's moat
Is only the warder's random shot;
Put off, put off, and row with speed,
For now is the time and the hour of need!

Those pond'rous keys* shall the kelpie's keep,
And lodge in their caverns dark and deep;
Nor shall Lochleven's towers or hall,
Hold our lovely lady Queen in thrall;
Or be the haunt of traitors, sold—
While Scotland has hands and hearts so bold;
Then steersman, steersman, on with speed,
For now is the time and the hour of need!

Hark! the alarm-bell hath rung,
And the warder's voice hath "Treason!" sung;
The echoes to the falconets roar,
Chime softly to the dashing oar.
Let town and hall, and battlements gleam,
We steer by the light of the taper's beam.
For "Scotland and Mary!" on with speed,
For now is the time, and the hour of need!

MARY.

IF there's a word that whispers love
    In gentlest tones to hearts of woe,
If there's a name more prized above
    And loved with deeper love below,
                'Tis Mary.

---

*The keys of her prison; since found in the lake.

If there's a healing sound beneath,
　To soothe the heart in sorrow's hour,
If there's a name that angels breathe,
　In silence with a deeper power,
　　　　　'Tis Mary.

It softly hangs on many a tongue,
　In lady's bower and sacred fane;
The sweetest name by poets sung,
　The high and consecrated strain,
　　　　　Is Mary.

And Scotia's Bard—life's holiest dream
　Was his, the silent heavens above,
When on the Bible o'er the stream,
　He vowed his early vows of love
　　　　　To Mary.

Oh, with the sweet repose of even,
　By forest lone, by fragrant lea;
And by thy beauties all, Loch Leven,
　How dear shall the remembrance be
　　　　　Of Mary.

Scotland and Mary are entwined
　With blooming wreath of fadeless green,
And printed on the undying mind,
　For, oh! her fair, though fated Queen
　　　　　Was Mary.

By the lone forest and the lea,
　　When smiles the thoughtful evening star
Though other names may nearer be
　　The sweetest, gentlest, loveliest far
　　　　　Is Mary!

MARY'S WEDDING.

YOU are to be married, Mary,
　　This hour as I wakeful lie,
In the dreamy hours of the morning,
　　Your wedding hour draws nigh.
Miles off, you are rising, dressing,
　　Your bride-maidens gay among,
In the same old house we played in
　　When you and I were young.

I can not call up your face, Mary,
　　The face of the bride to-day;
You have outgrown my knowledge,
　　The years have so slipped away.
I see but your girlish likeness,
　　Brown eyes, and brown falling hair
God knows I did love you dearly
　　And was proud that you were fair.

Many now speak my name, Mary,
    While yours in home's silence lies;
The future I read in toil's guerdon,
    You will read in your children's eyes.
The past—the same past with either—
    Is to you a delightsome scene,
But I can not trace it clearly
    For the graves that rise between.

I am glad *you* are happy, Mary,
    These tears could you see them fall
Would show, though you have forgotten,
    I have remembered all.
And though my cup may be empty
    While yours is all running o'er,
Heaven keep you its sweetness, Mary,
    And brimming forevermore.

MARY'S DREAM.

THE moon had climbed the highest hill,
    Which rises o'er the source of Dee,
And from the eastern summit shed
    Her silver light on tower and tree;
When Mary laid her down to sleep,
    Her thoughts on Sandy far at sea;
When soft and low a voice was heard,
    Say, "Mary, weep no more for me."

She from her pillow gently raised
   Her head, to ask who there might be—
She saw young Sandy shivering stand,
   With visage pale and hollow e'e;
" O, Mary dear! cold is my clay,
   It lies beneath a stormy sea;
Far, far from thee, I sleep in death;
   So Mary, weep no more for me!

Three stormy nights and stormy days,
   We tossed upon the raging main;
And long we strove our bark to save,
   But all our striving was in vain.
E'en then, when horror chilled my blood,
   My heart was filled with love for thee;
The storm is past, and I at rest;
   So, Mary, weep no more for me!

O! maiden dear, thyself prepare,
   We soon shall meet upon that shore
Where love is free from doubt and care,
   And thou and I shall part no more."
Loud crowed the cock, the shadow fled,
   No more of Sandy could she see;
But soft the passing spirit said,
   " Sweet Mary, weep no more for me!"

                JOHN LOWE.

MARY—THE ROSE OF ALLENDALE.

THE morn was fair, the skies were clear
　　No breath came o'er the sea
When Mary left her highland cot,
　　And wandered forth with me.
The flowers decked the mountain side,
　　And fragrance filled the vale,
By far the sweetest flower there
　　Was the Rose of Allendale.

Where'er I wandered east or west
　　Though fate began to lower
A solace still was she to me,
　　In sorrow's lonely hour.
When tempests lashed our gallant bark
　　And rent her shiv'ring sail,
One maiden form withstood the storm
　　'Twas the Rose of Allendale.

And when my fevered lips were parched
　　On Afric's burning sand,
The whispered hopes of happiness
　　And tales of distant land.
My life had been a wilderness
　　Unblest by fortune's gale
Had fate not linked my lot to her's,
　　The Rose of Allendale.

CHARLES JEFFRIES.

PRETTY MARY OF LOCH DAN.

THE shades of eve had crossed the glen
    That frowns o'er infant Avonmore,
When nigh Loch Dan, two weary men,
    We stopped before a cottage door.

"God save all here," my comrade cries,
    And rattles on the raised latch-pin;
"God save you kindly," quick replies
    A dear sweet voice, and asks us in.

We enter; from the wheel she starts,
    A rosy girl with soft black eyes;
Her fluttering court'sy takes our hearts,
    Her blushing grace, and pleased surprise.

Poor Mary she was quite alone,
    For all the way to Glenmalure,
Her mother had that morning gone,
    And left the house in charge with her.

She brought us in a beechen bowl,
    Sweet milk that smacked of mountain thyme,
Oat cake, and such a yellow roll
    Of butter—it gilds all my rhyme.

And while we ate the grateful food
   With weary limbs on bench reclined.
Considerate and discreet she stood
   Apart, and listened to the wind.

Kind wishes both our souls engaged,
   From breast to breast spontaneous ran
The mutual thought—we stood and pledged
   " The Modest Rose above Loch Dan."

" The milk we drink is not more pure,
   Sweet Mary, bless those budding charms!
Than your own generous heart, I'm sure,
   Nor whiter than the breast it warms!"

She turned and gazed, unused to hear
   Such language in that lonely glen,
But Mary you have naught to fear,
   Though smiled on by two wandering men.

Her simple heart could not but feel
   The words we spoke were free from guile;
She stooped, she blushed, she fixed her wheel—
   'Tis all in vain, she can't but smile!

Just like sweet April's dawn appears
   Her modest face—I see it yet,
And though I lived a hundred years,
   Methinks I never could forget.

For such another smile, I vow,
    Though loudly beats the midnight rain,
I'd take the mountain side e'en now,
    And walk to lone Loch Dan again!
                              SIR SAMUEL FERGUSON.

TO MARY.

(ON RECEIVING HER PICTURE).

THIS faint resemblance of thy charms,
    Though storng as mortal art could give,
My constant heart of fears disarms,
    Revives my hope, and bids me live.

Here I can trace the locks of gold,
    Which round thy snowy forehead wave,
The cheek, which sprung from Beauty's mold,
    The lips which made me Beauty's slave.

Here I can trace—ah, no! that eye,
    Whose azure floats in liquid fire,
Must all the painter's art defy
    And bid him from the task retire.

Here I behold its beauteous hue;
    But where's the beam so sweetly straying,
Which gave a lustre to its blue,
    Like Luna o'er the ocean playing.

Sweet copy! far more dear to me,
  Lifeless, unfeeling as thou art,
Than all the living forms could be,
  Save her, who placed thee next my heart.

She placed it, sad, with needless fear,
  Lest time might shake my wavering soul,
Unconscious that her image there,
  Held every sense in fast control.

Through hours, through years, through time, 'twill cheer;
  My hope, in gloomy moments, raise;
In life's last conflict 'twill appear,
  And meet my fond expiring gaze.

LORD BYRON.

HEROD'S LAMENT FOR MARIAMNE.

The following poem, by Lord Byron, refers to the historical fact that King Herod, having in a fit of jealous passion ordered the execution of his Queen Mariamne, on the charge of treason, was afterwards seized with uncontrollable remorse: knowing that she was entirely innocent, of that or any other crime.

OH! Mariamne! now for thee
　　The heart for which thou bled'st is bleeding;
Revenge is lost in agony,
　　And wild remorse to rage succeeding.
Oh, Mariamne! where art thou?
　　Thou canst not hear my bitter pleading:
Ah! could'st thou—*thou* would'st pardon now,
　　Though Heaven were to my prayer unheeding.

And is she dead?—and did they dare
　　Obey my phrenzy's jealous raving?
My wrath but doomed my own despair,
　　The sword that smote her's o'er me waving.
But thou art cold my murdered love!
　　And this dark heart is vainly craving
For her who soars alone above,
　　And leaves my soul, unworthy saving.

She's gone who shared my diadem;
　　She sunk, with her my joys entombing,
I swept that flower from Judah's stem,
　　Whose leaves for me alone were blooming,

And mine's the guilt, and mine's the hell,
  This bosom desolating—dooming;
And I have earned those tortures well
  Which unconsumed, are still consuming.
               HON. GEORGE NOEL BYRON.

BLUE-EYED MARY.

(AN OLD SONG TO GERMAN MUSIC).

"COME tell me blue-eyed stranger
    Say whither dost thou roam?
O'er this wide world a stranger
  Hast thou no friends, no home?"
    "They called me 'blue-eyed Mary,'
      When friends and fortune smiled
    But ah! how fortunes vary
      I now am sorrow's child."

"Come here, I'll buy thy flowers,
  And ease thy hapless lot,
Still wet with vernal showers
  I'll buy 'forget-me-not.'"
    "Kind sir, then take these posies
      They're fading like my youth
    But never, like these roses
      Shall wither Mary's truth."

" Look up, thou poor forsaken,
    I'll give thee house and home,
And if I'm not mistaken,
    Thou'lt never wish to roam."
        " Once more I'm 'Happy Mary'
          Once more has fortune smiled;
        Who ne'er from virtue vary
          May yet be Fortune's child.

"O MARY! CALL THE CATTLE HOME."

(OR MARY'S FATE ON THE SANDS OF DEE).

O MARY! go and call the cattle home,
      And call the cattle home,
And call the cattle home
      Across the sands of Dee.
  The western wind was wild and dank
  The western wind was wild and dank
Was wild and dank with foam;
      And all alone went she.

The creeping tide came up along the sand,
And o'er, and o'er the sand,
And round, and round the sand,
      As far as eye could see;

The blinding mist came pouring down,
The blinding mist came pouring down,
Came down and hid the land,
    And never home came she!

Oh! is it weed, or fish, or floating hair!
A tress o' golden hair!
O' drowned maiden's hair,
    Above the nets at sea?
    Was never weed or fish that shone,
That shone so fair
    Among the stakes on Dee!

They rowed her in across the rolling foam,
The cruel, crawling foam,
The cruel, hungry foam,
    To her grave beside the sea;
    But still the boatmen hear her call
    But still the boatmen hear her call
Call the cattle home
    Across the sands o' Dee.

                    CHARLES KINGSLEY.

A DAY DREAM OF MARY.

MY eyes make pictures when they're shut;
    I see a fountain large and fair,
A willow, and a ruined hut,
   And thee, and me, and Mary there.
     O! Mary make thy gentle lap our pillow,
     Bend o'er us like a bower my beautiful green willow!

A wild rose roofs the ruined shed
   And that and summer will agree;
And lo! where Mary leans her head
   Two dear names carved upon the tree:
     And Mary's tears they are not tears of sorrow,
     Our sister and our friends will both be here to-morrow!

      *   *   *   *   *   *

Thine eye-lash on my cheek doth play
   'Tis Mary's hand upon my brow!
But let me check this tender lay—
   Which none may hear, but she and thou;
     Like the still hive at quiet midnight humming,
     Murmur it to yourselves ye two beloved women!
                     SAMUEL T. COLERIDGE.

MARY'S TEAR.

(A QUAINT FANCY OF CRASHAW'S).

W HAT bright, soft thing is this,
　　Sweet Mary? thy fair eyes expense?
A moist spark it is.
　A watery diamond! from whence
　　The very term I think was found
　　The *water* of a diamond!

O 'tis not a tear,
　'Tis a star, about to drop
From thine eye, its sphere;
　The sun will stoop and take it up,
　　Proud will his sister be, to wear
　　This, thine eye's jewel in her ear!

　　*　　*　　*　　*　　*　　*

Fair drop, why quakest thou so?
　'Cause thou straight must lay thy head
In the dust?　O no,
　The dust shall never be thy bed.
　　A pillow for thee will I bring,
　　Stuffed with down of angel's wing.

Thus, carried up on high
　(For to Heaven thou must go),
Sweetly thou shalt lie,
　And in soft slumbers bathe thy woe;

Till the singing orbs awake thee,
    And one of their bright chorus make thee!

There thyself shalt be
    An eye; but not a weeping one,
Yet I doubt of thee,
    Whether thou hadst rather there have shone.
        An eye of Heaven; or still shine here
        In the Heaven of Mary's eye, a tear?

THE DEATH OF MARY.

IF I had thought thou could'st have died,
    I might not weep for thee,
But I forgot when by thy side
    That thou could'st mortal be;
It never through my mind had passed,
    That Time would ere be o'er—
When I on thee should look my last,
    And thou should'st smile no more.

And still upon that face I look
    And think 'twill smile again;
And still the thought I can not brook
    That I must look in vain;
But when I speak, thou dost not say
    What thou *ne'er left unsaid;*
And now I feel, as well I may
    Sweet Mary—thou art dead.

                              CHARLES WOLFE.

AN EPITAPH ON MARY DUTCHESS OF NORTHUMBERLAND.

UNDERNEATH this sable hearse
    Lies, the subject of all verse,
Sidney's sister, Pembroke's mother
DEATH! ere thou hast slain another,
Learned, fair and good as she,
TIME shall throw a dart at thee!

The above lines, as they are themselves deathless, defy Death; they were written by Johnson on Mary, daughter of **Sir Henry Sidney**, and wife of John Dudley, Duke of Northumberland.

TO MARY UNWIN.

MARY, I want a lyre with other strings;
    Such aid from Heaven as some have feigned to draw;
An eloquence scarce given to mortals, new
   And undefiled by praise of meaner things!
   That 'ere through age or woe I shed my wings,
I may record thy worth with honor due
In verse as musical as thou art true—
   Verse that immortalizes whom it sings!

But thou hast little need.   There is a Book
   By seraphs writ with beams of heavenly light;
On which the eyes of GOD, not rarely look
   A chronicle of actions just and bright!
     There all thy deeds, my faithful Mary shine,
     And since thou own'st that praise, I spare thee mine.
               WILLIAM COWPER.

TO MARY DEPARTED.

I SAW thy form in youthful prime,
    Nor thought that pale decay
Would steal before the steps of Time,
    And waste its bloom away, Mary!
Yet still thy features wore that light,
    Which fleets not with the breath;
And life ne'er looked more truly bright
    Than in thy smile of death, Mary!

As streams that run o'er golden mines,
    Yet humbly, calmly glide,
Nor seem to know the wealth that shines
    Within their gentle tide, Mary!
So veiled beneath the simplest guise,
    Thy radient genius shone,
And that which charmed all other eyes
    Seemed worthless in thine own, Mary!

If souls could always dwell alone,
    Thou ne'er had'st left that sphere,
Or could we keep the souls we love,
    We ne'er had'st lost thee here, Mary!
Though many a gifted mind we meet,
    Though fairest forms we see,
To live with them is far less sweet
    Than to remember thee, Mary!

HER SMILE I SHALL NEVER FORGET.

FAREWELL, my dear Mary, the beams of thy beauty
    No longer shall brighten the path I pursue,
For loud on the blast rolls the mandate of duty,
    And glory bids pleasure and Mary adieu;
But though, lovely maid, it seems madness to lose thee,
    Yet absence shall soften the sigh of regret,
For memory pledges, when fondly it woos thee,
    Thy smile, thy sweet smile, I shall never forget.

Farewell, my first love, but the tear that's now falling
    Preserve as a relic, a relic from me;
And each lonely hour my affection recalling,
    That heart-drop of sorrow thy lover shall be;
And when thou hast brought my lost image before thee,
    Let memory soften the sigh of regret,
For the tear shall declare I must ever adore thee,
    And thy smile, thy sweet smile, I shall never forget.

Farewell, then forever, the night star that listens,
    My vows may record in the temples above
And the last parting tear, in the moonbeam that glistens,
    Shall stamp as a seal, the sweet bond of my love;
For I swear, till the night of the tomb overtake me,
    And the sun of my life shall forever be set,
My fondness for Mary shall never forsake me
    And her smile, her sweet smile, I shall *never* forget!

MARY'S TRIBUTE OF TEARS.

O! MARY, when morn breaks and brightens the hour,
    And gilds the green waves of the sea,
My mem'ry wonders away to the bower
    That was sacred to love and to thee;
And then my sad spirit doth mournfully rove,
    Round the spot to my bosom so dear,
Fondly tracing the scenes of our earliest love,
    Till remembrance awakens—the tear.

O! Mary, whene'er I see night coming on,
    And the sunbeams are hast'ning away,
I think of the scenes that forever are gone,
    And sunk, like the orb of the day;
Then, then my sad spirit doth mournfully rove,
    Round the spot to my bosom so dear,
Fondly tracing each scene of our earliest love,
    Till remembrance awakens—the tear.

O! Mary, whenever the moon I behold
    As in splendor she sails through the sky,
I think, oh! how swift the bright seasons have rolled,
    And how fast the soft pleasures flew by;
And then my sad spirit doth mournfully rove
    Round the spot to my bosom so dear,
Fondly tracing each scene of our earliest love,
    Till remembrance awakens—the tear.

DESPAIR FOR MARY.

(AIR: GRAMACHEE).

O! TAKE me to yon sunny isle
　　That stands in Fortha's sea,
For there all lonely, I may weep
　　Since tears my lot must be.
The caverned rocks alone shall hear
　　My anguish and my woe,
But can their echoes Mary bring?
　　Ah! no, no, no!

I'll wander by the silent shore,
　　Or climb the rocky steep,
And list to ocean murmering
　　The music of the deep;
But when the soft moon lights the wave
　　In evening's silver glow,
Shall Mary meet me 'neath its light
　　Ah! no, no, no!

I'll speak of her to every flower—
　　And lovely flowers are there,
They'll maybe bow their heads and weep
　　For she, like them was fair;
And every bird I'll teach a song
　　A plaintive song of woe,
But Mary, can she hear their strains?
　　Ah! no, no, no!

MARY WILL SMILE AGAIN.

THE morn was fresh, and pure the gale,
    When Mary from her cot a rover,
Plucked many a wild rose of the vale
    To bind the temples of her lover,
As near his little farm she strayed
    Where birds of love were ever praising,
She saw her William in the shade—
    The arms of ruthless war preparing.
"Though now" he cried "I seek the hostile plain,
Mary shall smile, and all be fair again."

She seized his hand, and "Ah!" she cried
    "Wilt thou, to camps and war a stranger,
Desert thy Mary's faithful side,
    And bare thy life to every danger?
Yet go, brave youth! to arm away!
    My maiden hands for fight shall dress thee,
And when the drum beats far away
    I'll drop a silent tear and bless thee."
Return'd with honor from the hostile plain,
Mary will smile, and all be fair again.

"The bugles through the forest wind,
    The woodland soldiers call to battle,
Be some protecting angel kind,
    And guard thy life when cannons rattle!"

She sung—and as the rose appears
  In sunshine, when the storm is over,
A smile beamed sweetly through her tears—
  The blush of promise to her lover;
Returned in triumph from the hostile plain
All shall be fair and Mary smile again.

MARY CHUISLE.*

Among the ancient Bardic poetry of Celtic tradition is found the following forcible though crude thoughts of an unknown author: for strong imagry the last line is unsurpassed by any poet, in any language.

O MARY CHUISLE! blossom of fairness,
    Branch of generousness, westward from the Nair,
Whose voice is sweeter than the cuckoo's on the branch,
You have left me in the anguish of death.
    The candle is not close to me, the table nor the company,
    From the soul-faintness you cause me: O! star of woman.
    Majestic graceful maid, who has increased my woe,
    Alas, that I am without your cloak till dawn!

I have walked to Ardagh and Kinsale,
To Drogheda and back again,
To Carlow and Downpatrick,—
I have not looked upon the like of Mary.

---
*Chuisle—a term of endearment.

High coaches have I seen and white horses,
And English cavaliers fighting for their ladies;
If you go home from me Mary—"safe home to you,"
Your shadow would make light without the sun!

(TRANS. FOR "POETS AND POETRY OF IRELAND").

A MONASTIC TRIBUTE TO MARY.

(FROM THE CELTIC).

MURDOCH, whet thy knife, that we may shave our crowns to the Great King:
Let us sweetly give our vow, and the hair of both our heads
   to the Trinity.
"No: I will shave mine to Mary—this is the doing of a true
   heart,
To Mary shave thou these locks, thou well-formed, soft-eyed
   man.

    *   *   *   *   *   *

Seldom hast thou had, handsome man, a knife on thy hair,
   to shave it:
Oftener has a sweet, soft queen combed her hair beside thee;
Ua Chais and I strove in a race—these two knives, one to
   each,
Were given us by Duncan Cairbreach;
No knives of knives were better; shave gently then Murdoch.

*   *   *   *   *   *

Preserve our shaved heads from cold and from heat, gentle
daughter of Jodchim; (Joseph)
Preserve us in the land of heat, softest branch of Mary."

BISHOP EWING'S TRANSLATION.

MARIE LAGHAC.

(FROM THE GAELIC).

YOUNG was I and Mary
   In the windings of Glensmeoil,
When came that imp of Venus,
   And caught us with his wile,
And pierced us with his arrows
   That we thrilled in every pore,
And loved as mortals never loved
   On this green earth before.

CHORUS:

O! my bonnie Mary,
   My dainty love, and queen,
The fairest, rarest, Mary
   On earth was ever seen.
O! my queenly Mary
   That made a king of men,
To call thee my own, Mary,
   Born in the bonnie glen.

Oftimes myself and Mary
   Strayed up the bonnie glen;
Our hearts as pure and innocent
   As little children then.
Boy Cupid finely taught us,
   To dally and to toy,
When the shade fell from the green tree,
   And the sun was in the sky.

    CHORUS.—O! my bonnie Mary, &c.

If all the wealth of Albyn
   Were mine, and treasures rare,
What boots all gold and silver
   If the sweet love be not there?
More dear to me than rubies
   In deepest veins that shine,
Is one kiss from the lips
   That rightly I call mine.

    CHORUS.—O! my bonnie Mary, &c.

Thy bosom's heaving whiteness
   With beauty overbrims,
Like swan upon the waters
   When gentliest it swims;
Like cotton on the moorland,
   Thy skin is soft and fine,
Thy neck is like the sea gull,
   When dipping in the brine.

    CHORUS.—O! my bonnie Mary, &c.

The locks about thy dainty ear,
  Do richly curl and twine;
Dame Nature rarely grew a wealth
  Of ringlets, like to thine.
There needs no hand of hireling,
  To twist and plait thy hair,
But where it grew, it winds and falls,
  In wavey beauty there.

CHORUS.—O! my bonnie Mary, &c.

Like snow upon the mountains,
  Thy teeth are pure and white;
Thy breath is like the cinnamon
  Thy mouth buds with delight;
Thy cheeks are like the cherries,
  Thine eyelids soft and fair,
And smooth thy brow, untaught to frown,
  Beneath thy golden hair.

CHORUS.—O! my bonnie Mary, &c.

The pomp of mighty Kaisers
  Our state doth not surpass,
When 'neath the lofty coppice
  We lie upon the grass;
The purple flowers around us
  Outspread their rich array,
Where the lusty mountain streamlet,
  Is leaping from the brae.

CHORUS.—O! my bonnie Mary, &c.

Nor harp, nor pipe, nor organ,
  From touch of cunning men
Made music half so eloquent
  As our hearts thrilled with then;
When the blithe lark, lightly soaring,
  And the mavis on the spray,
And the cuckoo in the greenwood,
  Sang hymns to greet the May.

    CHORUS.—O! my bonnie Mary, &c.
        PROF. JOHN STUART BLACKIE.

THE EMIGRANT'S FAREWELL TO HIS MARY.

I'M sitting on the stile, Mary,
  Where we sat side by side,
On a bright May morning long ago,
  When first you were my bride.
The corn was springing fresh and green,
  And the lark sang loud and high,
And the red was on your lip, Mary,
  And the love light in your eye.

The place is little changed, Mary,
  The day's as bright as then;
The lark's loud song is in my ear,
  And the corn is green again.

But I miss the soft clasp of your hand,
  And your warm breath on my cheek,
And I still keep listening for the words
  You never more may speak.

'Tis but a step down yonder lane,
  The village church stands there,
The church where we were wed, Mary,
  I see the spire from here.
But the graveyard lies between, Mary,
  And my step might break your rest,
Where I've laid you darling, down to sleep
  With your baby on your breast.

I'm very lonely now, Mary,
  For the poor make no new friends;
But O, they love them better still
  The few our Father sends!
And you were all my pride, Mary,
  My blessing and my pride;
There's nothing left to care for now,
  Since my poor Mary died.

I'm bidding you a long farewell,
  My Mary kind and true;
But I'll not forget you, darling,
  In the land I'm going to.
They say there's bread and work for all,
  And the sun shines always there,
But I'll not forget my darling,
  Were she fifty times less fair.

LADY DUFFERIN.

MAIRE BHAN ASTOR.*

IN a valley far away,
  With my *Maire bhan astór*,
Short would be the summer day
  Ever loving more and more;
Winter days would all grow long,
  With the light her heart would pour,
With her kisses and her song,
  And her loving *mait go leor.*†
    Fond is Maire bhan astór,
    Fair is Maire bhan astór,
    Sweet as ripple on the shore,
    Sings my Maire bhan astór.

Oh! her sire is very proud,
  And her mother cold as stone;
But her brother bravely vowed,
  She should be my bride alone;
For he knew I loved her well,
  And he knew she loved me too,
So he sought their pride to quell
  But 'twas all in vain to sue.
    True is Maire bhan astór,
    Tried is Maire bhan astór,
    Had I wings, I'd never soar
    From my Maire bhan astor.

---

* Fair Mary, my treasure. † Much plenty, or in abundance.

There are lands where manly toil
  Surely reaps the crop it sows;
Glorious woods and teaming soil,
  Where the broad Missouri flows;
Through the trees the smoke shall rise,
  From our hearth with *mail go leór;*
There shall shine the happy eyes
  Of my Maire bhan astór.
      Mild is Maire bhan astór,
      Mine is Maire bhan astór,
      Saints will watch about the door,
      Of my Maire bhan astór!

THOMAS DAVIS.

LOVELY MARY DONNELLY.

O LOVELY Mary Donnelly, it's you I love the best!
    If fifty girls were round you, I'd hardly see the rest.
Be what it may the time of day, the place be where it will.
Sweet looks of Mary Donnelly, they bloom before me still.
Her eyes like mountain water that's flowing on a rock,
How clear they are, how dark they are, and they give me
    many a shock.
Red rowans warm in sunshine, and wetted with a shower,
Could ne'er express the charming lip that has me in its
    power.
O lovely Mary Donnelly, it's you I love the best!
If fifty girls were round you, I'd hardly see the rest.

The dance of last Whit-Monday night exceeded all before,
No pretty girl for miles around was missing from the floor;
But Mary kept the belt of love, and oh! but she was gay!
She danced so light, she sang a song that took my heart
    away.
When she stood up for dancing, her steps were so complete
The music nearly ceased itself, to listen to her feet;
The fiddler moaned his blindness, he heard her so much
    praised,
But blessed himself he wasn't deaf, when once her voice she
    raised.
O lovely Mary Donnelly, it's you I love the best!
If fifty girls were round you, I'd hardly see the rest.

O! you're the flower of womankind in country or in town;
The higher I exalt you, the lower I'm cast down,
If some great lord should come this way and see your
    beauty bright,
And you become his lady, I'd own it was but right.
O might we live together in lofty palace hall,
Where joyful music rises, where scarlet curtains fall!
Or might we live together in a cottage mean and small,
With sods of grass the only roof, and mud the only wall!
O lovely Mary Donnelly, your beauty's my distress.
Its far too beauteous to be mine, but I'll never wish it less;
The proudest place would fit your face, and I am poor and
    low,
But blessings be about you dear, wherever you may go.
                  WILLIAM ALLINGHAM.

THE FOUR MARIES.

(A SCOTCH BALLAD ATTRIBUTED TO MARY HAMILTON,
MAID OF HONOR TO QUEEN MARIE STUART).

LAST night the Queen had four Maries,
   This night there'll be but three;
There was Mary Beton, and Mary Seton,
   An' Mary Carmichael an' me.

Oh, little did my mither think,
   When first she cradled me,
That I should dee sae far from hame,
   An' dee on the gallows tree.

I charge ye, all ye mariners,
   When ye sail o'er the foam,
Let neither my father or mither get wit—
   But that I'm coming home.

For if my father an' mither get wit,
   And my bold brithers three,
O mickle would be the gude red bluid,
   This day would be spilt for me.

They'll tie a napkin round my een,
   An' they'll no let me see to dee,
An' they'll ne'er let on to my father an' mither,
   But I'm away o'er the sea.

I wish I could lie in our ain kirkyard,
    Aneath the auld yew tree:
Where we pu'd the gowans, an' thread the rowans—
    My brithers, my sisters and me.

But little care I for a nameless grave,
    If I've the hope for eternity:
So that the faith o' the deeing thief:
    May be granted through faith to me.

HIGHLAND MARY.

YE banks and braes and streams around
    The castle o' Montgomery!
Green be your woods and fair your flowers,
    Your waters never drum'lie.
There simmer first unfaulds her robes
    And there the longest tarry;
For there I took the last fareweel
    O' my sweet Highland Mary.

How sweetly bloomed the gay green birk,
    How rich the hawthorns blossom,
As underneath their fragant shade
    I clasped her to my bosom!

The golden hours on angel wings,
　Flew o'er me and my dearie;
For dear to me as light and life
　Was my sweet Highland Mary.

W'i mony a vow and locked embrace,
　Our parting was fu' tender;
And pledging oft to meet again,
　We tore oursel's asunder;
But oh! fell Death's untimely frost,
　That nipt my flower sae early!
Now greens the sod, and caulds the clay
　That wraps my Highland Mary.

O pale, pale now, those rosy lips
　I oft hae kissed sae fondly!
And closed for aye the sparkling glance
　That dwelt on me sae kindly;
And mould'ring now in silent dust,
　That heart that lo'ed me dearly!
But still within my bosom's core
　Shall live my Highland Mary.

ROBERT BURNS.

AFTON WATER.

(ADDRESSED TO HIS EARLY LOVE MARY).

FLOW gently sweet Afton among thy green braes,
Flow gently I'll sing thee a song in thy praise;
My Mary's asleep by thy murmering stream;
Flow gently sweet Afton, disturb not her dream.

How lofty sweet Afton, thy neighboring hills,
Far marked with the courses of clear winding rills;
There daily I wander as noon rises high,
My flocks and my Mary's sweet cot in my eye.

How pleasant thy banks, and green valleys below,
Where wild in the woodlands the primroses blow;
There oft, as mild ev'ning sweeps over the lea,
The sweet scented birks shade my Mary and me.

Thy crystal stream Afton, how lovely it glides,
And winds by the cot where my Mary resides;
How wanton thy waters, her snowy feet lave,
As gath'ring sweet flowerets she stems thy clear wave.

Flow gently sweet Afton, among thy green braes,
Flow gently sweet river, the theme of my lays;
My Mary's asleep by thy murmering stream,
Flow gently sweet Afton, disturb not her dream.

ROBERT BURNS.

TO MARY IN HEAVEN.

THOU ling'ring star, with less'ning ray,
  That lov'st to greet the early morn,
Again thou usher'st in the day,
  When Mary from my soul was torn.
O Mary! dear departed shade,
  Where is thy place of blissful rest?
See'st thou thy lover lowly laid,
  Hear'st thou the groans that rend his breast?

That sacred hour can I forget,
  Can I forget the hallowed grove?
Where by the winding Ayr we met
  To live one day of parting love!
Eternity can not efface
  Those records dear of transports past,
Thy image at our last embrace—
  Ah little thought we, 'twas our last!

Ayr, gurgling kissed his pebbled shore,
  O'er hung with wild woods thick'ning green,
The fragrant birch and hawthorne hoar,
  Twined amorous 'round the raptured scene;
The flowers sprang wanton to be pressed,
  The birds sang love on every spray;
Till too, too soon the glowing west
  Proclaim'd the speed of wingèd day.

Still o'er these scenes my mem'ry wakes,
    And fondly broods with miser care!
Time, but th' impression stronger makes,
    As streams their channels deeper wear,
My Mary, dear departed shade!
    Where is thy place of blissful rest?
See'st thou thy lover lowly laid,
    Hear'st thou the groans that rend his breast?

                              ROBERT BURNS.

WILL YE GO TO THE INDIES MY MARY?

WILL ye go to the Indies, my Mary
    And leave auld Scotia's shore?
Will ye go to the Indies, my Mary,
    Across the Atlantic's roar?

O sweet grows the lime and the orange
    And the apple on the pine;
But a' the charmes o' the Indies,
    Can never equal thine.

I hae sworn by the Heavens to my Mary,
    I hae sworn by the Heavens to be true;
And sae may the Heavens forget me
    When I forget my vow!

O plight me your faith my Mary,
  And plight me your lilly-white hand;
O plight me your faith my Mary
  Before I leave Scotia's strand.

We hae plighted our troth my Mary
  In mutual affection to join,
And curst be the cause that shall part us,
  The hour and the moment o' time!

ROBERT BURNS.

MY BONNIE MARY.*

GO fetch to me a pint o' wine
And fill it in a silver tassie,
That I may drink before I go
A service to my bonnie lassie;
The boat rocks at the pier o' Leith,
Fu' loud the wind blaws frae the Ferry,
The ship rides by the Berwick-law,
And I maun leave my bonnie Mary.

The trumpets sound, the banners fly,
The glittering spears are ranked and ready,
The shouts o' war are heard afar,
The battle closes deep and bloody:
It's not the roar o' sea or shore,
Wad' make me longer wish to tarry;
Nor shouts o' war thus heard afar,—
It's leaving thee, my bonnie Mary.

ROBERT BURNS.

---

* Probably some transient acquaintance who happened to strike the susceptible poet's fancy. "Mary," seems to have been with Burns as with many poets a favorite name.

WILL YE GO TO THE HIGHLANDS, MY MARY?

(AIR: GWE BUGHTS, MARION).

WILL ye go to the Highlan's, my Mary
    And visit our haughs and our glens?
There's beauty 'mang hills o' the Highlan's,
    The lass in the Lowlands, ne'er kens.

'Tis true we've few cowslips or roses,
    Nae lillies grow wild on the lea;
But the heather its sweet scent discloses,
    And the daisy's as sweet to the 'ee.

See yon far heathy hills, whare they're risin',
    Whose summits are shaded wi' blue;
There the fleet mountain roes are lyin',
    Or feeding their fawns love, for you.

Right sweet are our scenes in the gloamin',
    When shepherds return from the hill,
Around by the banks o' Loch Lomon,
    While bagpipes are soundin' sae shrill.

Right sweet are the low-setting sunbeams,
    That point o'er the quiv'ring stream;
But sweeter the smiles, o' my Mary,
    And kinder the blinks o' her een.

ROBERT BURNS.

MARY MORISON.

O MARY at thy window be,
   It is the wished, the trysted hour,
Those smiles and glances let me see,
   That make the miser's treasure poor;
How blithely wad I bide the stour,
   A weary slave frae sun to sun,
Could I the rich reward secure—
   The lovely Mary Morison!

Yestreen, when to the trembling string,
   The dance ga'ed thro' the lighted pa',
To thee my fancy took its wing,
   I sat but neither heard nor saw,
Tho' this was fair, and that was braw;
   And you the toast of a' the town
I sighed and said among them a',
   "Ye are na Mary Morison!"

O Mary can'st thou wreck his peace
   Wha for thy sake would gladly dee?
Or can'st thou break that heart of his
   Whose only faut is loving thee?
If love for love thou wilt na gie,
   At least be pity to me shown
A thought ungentle canna be
   The thought o' Mary Morison!

ROBERT BURNS.

THE EMIGRANT'S LETTER TO MARY.

MY young heart's love, twelve years have been
    A century to me,
I have not seen thy smile, nor heard
    Thy voice's melody.
The many hardships I've endured,
    Since I left Larock lea,
I must not tell, for it would bring
    The salt tear in thine 'ee.

But I have news, and happy news,
    To tell unto my love—
What I have won, to me more dear,
    That it my heart can prove.
Its thoughts, unchanged, still it is true,
    And surely so is thine;
Thou never, never can'st forget
    That two were one—lang syne!

The summer sun looks on the tarn,
    And on the primrose brae,
Where we, in days of innocence
    Were wont to sport and play.
And I among the mossy springs
    Wade for the honey-blooms;
For thee, the rush tiara wove,
    Bedecked with lily plumes.

When on the ferney knoll we sat,
    A happy, happy pair,
Thy comely cheek laid on my knee,
    I braid thy golden hair.
Oh, then I felt the holiest thought
    That entered e'er my mind—
If Mary was to be to me,
    Forever true and kind.

Though fair the flowers that bloom around
    My dwelling o'er the sea,
Though bright the streams, and green the bowers,
    They are not so to me.
I hear the bulbuls mellow song,
    Upon the gorgeous palm,
The sweet chirp of the feathered bee
    Among the fields of baslm.

But there are no old country birds,
    So dear to childhood's days—
The laveroch, linnet, thrush and lark,
    That taught us love's sweet lays.
And when thou walk'st alone, to think
    On him that's o'er the sea,
Their cheerful, soft love-notes will tell,
    My heart's love-thoughts to thee.

Let joy be in thy leal heart,
    And bright smiles in thy 'ee—
The bonnie bark is In the bay;
    I'm coming home to thee!

I'm coming home to thee, Mary,
    With many a jewel fine,
And I will lay them in thy lap,
    For the kiss of sweet langsyne!

AVE MARIA.

(THE OUTLAW'S PRAYER TO MARY).

AVE MARIA, maiden mild!
    Listen to a maiden's prayer;
Thou can'st hear though from the wild,
    Thou can'st save amid despair.
Safe may we sleep beneath thy care,
    Though banish'd, outcast and reviled,
Maiden, hear a maiden's prayer,
    Mother, hear a suppliant child!
                    Ave Maria!

Ave Maria! undefiled!
    The flinty couch we now must share,
Shall seem with down of eider piled,
    If thy protection hover there.
The murky cavern's heavy air,
    Shall breathe of balm if thou has smiled;
Then maiden hear a maiden's prayer,
    Mother list a suppliant child!
                    Ave Maria!

Ave Maria! stainless styled!
  Foul demons of the earth and air,
From this, their wonted haunt exiled
  Shall flee before thy presence fair,
We bow us to our lot of care,
  Beneath thy guidance, reconciled;
Hear for a maid, a maiden's prayer;
  And for a father hear a child!
           Ave Maria!
             SIR WALTER SCOTT.

NORMAN'S SONG TO MARY.

(FROM THE LADY OF THE LAKE).

THE heath this night must be my bed,
  The bracken, curtain for my head,
My lullaby the warder's tread,
      Far, far from love and thee, Mary!

To-morrow eve, more stilly laid,
My couch may be my bluidy plaid,
My vesper song, thy wail sweet maid!
      It will not waken me, Mary!

I may not, dare not, fancy now,
The grief that clouds thy lovely brow,
I dare not think upon my vow,
      And all it promised me, Mary!

No fond regret must Norman know,
When bursts Clan-Alpin on the foe,
His heart must be like bended bow,
  His foot, like arrow free, Mary!

A time will come with feeling fraught,
For if I fall in battle fought,
The hapless lover's dying thought
  Shall be a thought on thee, Mary.

And if return'd from conquer'd foes;
How blythly will the evening close,
How sweet the linnet-song repose
  To my young bride and me, Mary!
      SIR WALTER SCOTT.

MY MARY DEAR.

(TUNE: ANNIE LAURIE).

THE gloamin' star was showerin'
  Its siller glories doun,
And nestled in its mossy lair
 The lintie sleepit soun',
 The lintie sleepit soun',
And the starnies sparkled clear,
When on a gowany bank I sat,
Aside my Mary dear.

The burnie wanders eerie
Roun' rock and ruin'd tower,
By mony a fairy hillock
And mony a lanely bower;
Roun' mony a lanely bower,
Love's tender tale to hear,
Where I in whisper'd vows ha'e woo'd
And won my Mary dear.

Oh, hallow'd hours o' happiness
Frae me forever ta'en!
Wi' summer's flow'ry loveliness
Ye come na' back again!
Ye come na' back again,
The waefu' heart to cheer,
For lang the greedy grave has closed
Aboun my Mary dear!

MARY.

I N life's gay morn when hope beats high,
   And youthfu' love's endearing tie,
Gave rapture to the mutual sigh,
      Within the arms of Mary,
      My ain dear Mary;
Nae joys beneath the vaulted sky
      Could equal mine wi' Mary.

The sacred hours like moments flew,
Soft transports thrill'd my bosom through,
The warl' evanish'd fra my view,
    Within the arms of Mary,
    My ain dear Mary;
Nae glooming cares my soul e'er knew,
    Within the arms of Mary.

Young fancy spread her visions gay,
Love fondly view'd the fair display,
Hope show'd the blissfu' nuptial day,
    And I was rapt with Mary;
    My ain dear Mary.
The flowers of Eden strew'd the way
    That led me to my Mary.

But life is now a dreary waste,
I lanely wander sair depress'd,
For cold and lifeless is that breast
    Where throbb'd the heart of Mary,
    My ain dear Mary;
She's gane to seats o' blissfu' rest,
    And I ha'e lost my Mary.

MARY AT THE BURN.

WHEN trees did bud and fields were green
    And broom bloomed fair to see,
When Mary was complete fifteen
    And love laughed in her e'e.

Now Davy did each lad surpass
    That dwelt at this burnside,
And Mary was the bonniest lass
    Just meet to be a bride.

Her cheeks were rosy red and white,
    Her een were bonny blue,
Her locks were like Aurora bright,
    Her lips like dropping dew.

As down the burn they took their way,
    And through the flowery dale,
His cheek to her's he oft did lay,
    And love was aye the tale.

With, "Mary, when shall we return,
    Sic pleasure to renew?"
Quoth Mary, "Love I like the burn,
    And aye will follow you."

                    ROBERT CRAWFORD.

MARY DHU.

SWEET, sweet is the rose-bud
    Bathed in dew;
But sweeter art thou
    My Mary Dhu.
Oh! the skies of night,
With their eyes of light,
Are not so bright
    As my Mary.
Whenever thy radiant face I see,
The clouds of sorrow depart from me:
    As the shadows fly,
    From day's bright eye,
    Thou lightest life's sky
      My Mary Dhu.

Sad, sad is my heart
    When I sigh adieu!
Or gaze on thy parting,
    My Mary Dhu!
Then for thee I mourn
Till thy steps return,
Bids my bosom burn—
    My Mary Dhu!
I think but of thee on the brown-clad hills,
I muse but on thee by the moorland rills

In the morning light,
In the moonshine bright,
Thou art still in my sight,
  My Mary Dhu.

Thy voice trembles through me,
    Like the breeze
That ripples in gladness
    The leafy trees;
'Tis a wafted tone,
From Heaven's high throne,
Making hearts thine own,
    My Mary Dhu.
Be the flowers of joy ever round thy feet
With colors glowing, and incense sweet;
    And when thou must away,
    May life's rose decay
    In the west winds sway—
        My Mary Dhu.
                    DAVID MACBETH MOIR.

MARY OF ARGYLE.

I HAVE heard the mavis singing
　His love song to the morn;
I have seen the dew-drops clinging
　To the rose, just newly born—
But a sweeter song has cheered me,
　At the evening's gentle close;
And I've seen an eye still brighter
　Than the dew-drop on the rose;
'Twas thy voice, my gentle Mary,
　And thine artless, winning smile,
That made this world an Eden—
　Bonnie Mary of Argyle.

Though thy voice may lose its sweetness,
　And thine eye its brightness too;
Though thy step may lose its fleetness,
　And thy hair its sunny hue;
Still to me wilt thou be dearer
　Than all the world shall own,
I have loved thee for thy beauty
　But not for that alone;
I have watched thy heart, dear Mary,
　And its goodness was the wile,
That has made thee mine forever,
　Bonnie Mary of Argyle!

                                    CHARLES JEFFRIES.

MY AIN MY ARTLESS MARY.

(OR, "MEET ME ON THE GOWAN LEA.")

MEET me on the gowan lea,
  Bonnie Mary, sweetest Mary;
Meet me on the gowan lea,
  My ain, my artless Mary.

Before the sun sinks in the west,
And nature a' ha'e gane to rest,
There to my fond, my faithful breast,
  Oh, let me clasp my Mary.

> Meet me on the gowan lea, &c.

The gladsome lark o'er moor and fell,
The lintie in the bosky dell,
Nae blyther than your bonnie sel'
  My ain, my artless Mary.

> Meet me on the gowan lea, &c.

We'll join our love notes to the breeze
That sighs in whispers through the trees,
And a' that twa fond hearts can please
  Will be our song, dear Mary.

> Meet me on the gowan lea, &c.

There ye shall sing the sun to rest,
While to my faithfu' bosom prest;
Then wha sae happy, wha sae blest,
    As me and my dear Mary.

Meet me on the gowan lea!
    Bonnie Mary, sweetest Mary,
Meet me on the gowan lea,
    My ain, my artless Mary!

MARY.

(AIR: THE FLOWER OF DUNBLANE).

HOW saft sink the shadows when day disappearing,
    Behind yon grey mountain bids Tarland adieu!
While clouds to the western horizon are steering,
    And sunsets bright glories yet linger in view.
Oh! fair fa' the gloamin' when Mary is roaming,
    The cantie bit lassie that dearly I lo'e;
Oh! fair fa' the gloamin', where torrents are foaming
    A-down the steep rocks on the braes o' Ben Dhu!

She treads the rich clover, where each painted rover—
    Bright butterflies—sported the long summer day;
She plucks the red brier rose—the woodbine its lover,
    And twines her dark locks ur' the white-blossom'd May.

Oh! fair fa' the gloamin' when Mary is roaming
　'Mid braw luckan gowans and harebells sae blue;
Oh! fair fa' the gloamin' where torrents are foaming
　A-down the wild corries and craigs o' Ben Dhu!

Among the rough copsewood, across the green paling,
　Through meadow-sweet, fair as the pearl-blossom'd spray,
Where birches in tears, are their fragrance exhaling,
　As light as the roe-deer she bounds on her way.
Oh! fair fa' the gloamin' when Mary is roaming
　Sae winsome and bonnie, sae gentle and true;
My steps fly to meet her, and soon shall I greet her—
　The joy of my fond heart! the pride of Ben Dhu!

MARIA D. OGILOY.

OUR MARY.*

("OR, MARY SWEET WEE WOMAN.")

OUR Mary liket weel to stray
　　Where clear the burn was rowin
And troth she was, though I it say,
As fair as aught ere made o' clay,
　And pure as ony gowan,

And happy too, as ony lark
　The clud might ever carry;
She shunn'd the ill, and sought the good,
E'en mair than weel was understood,
　And a' folk liket Mary.

---

* From Riddles ballad " The Cottage of Glendale."

But she fell sick ur' some decay
   When she was but eleven;
And as she pined from day to day,
We grudged to see her gaun away,
   Though she was gaun to Heaven.

   *   *   *   *   *   *

But Mary had a gentle heart—
   Heaven did as gently free her;
Yet lang afore she reach'd that part,
Dear Sir it wad ha'e made ye start,
   Had ye been there to see her.

Sae changed, and yet sae sweet and fair
   And growing meek and meeker,
Wi' her lang locks o' yellow hair
She wore a little angel's air,
   Ere angels came to seek her.

And when she could not stray out by,
   The wee wild flowers to gather
She oft her household plays wad try
To hide her illness frae our eye,
   Lest she should grieve us farther,

And ilka thing we said or did
   Aye pleased the sweet wee creature;
Indeed ye wad ha'e thought she had,
A something in her made her glad,
   Ayont the course of nature.

   *   *   *   *   *   *

But death's cauld hour came on at last,
  As it to a' is commin;
And may it be, whene'er it falls
Nae waur to others than it was
  To Mary, sweet wee woman!

BONNIE MARY.

WHEN the sun gaes down, when the sun gaes down,
  I'll meet thee bonnie Mary, when the sun gaes down,
I'll row my apron up, an' I'll leave the reeky town,
And meet thee by the burnie, when the sun gaes down.

  When the sun gaes down, &c.

By the burnie, there's a bower, we will gently lean us there,
An' forget in ither's arms every earthly care,
For the chiefest o' my joys, in this weary mortal roun',
Is the burnside wi' Mary when the sun gaes down.

  When the sun gaes down, &c.

There the ruin'd castle tower on the distant steep appears,
Like a hoary auld warrior faded with years,
An' the burnie stealing by wi' a fairy silver soun',
Will sooth us with its music when the sun gaes down.

  When the sun gaes down, &c.

The burnside is sweet when the dew is on the flower,
But 'tis like a little heaven at the trystin' hour,
And with pity I would look on the king who wears the crown,
When wi' thee by the burnie, when the sun gaes down.

When the sun gaes down, &c.

When the sun gaes down, when the sun gaes down,
I'll meet thee by the burnie, when the sun gaes down;
Come in thy petticoatie, and thy little drugget gown,
And I'll meet thee bonnie Mary when the sun gaes down.

When the sun gaes down, &c.

I'D EVER KEEP MY MARY.

"(ALONG BY SEVERN STREAM SO CLEAR.)"

ALONG by Severn stream so clear,
   When spring adorns the infant year,
And music charms the list'ning ear
   I'll wandar with my Mary,
   My bonnie blooming Mary;
Not Spring itsself to me is dear
   When absent from my Mary.

When summer's sun pours on my head,
His sultry rays, I'll seek the shade,
Unseen, upon a primrose bed,

I'll sit with little Mary,
My bonny blooming Mary;
Where fragrant flowers are spread
To charm my little Mary.

She's mild's the sun through April show'r
That glances on the leafy bower
She's sweet as Flora's fav'rite flower
My bonny little Mary,
My blooming little Mary,
Give me but her, no other dower
I'll ask with little Mary.

Should fickle fortune frown on me,
And leave me bare's the naked tree,
Possessed of her, how rich I'd be
My lovely little Mary,
My bonny blooming Mary;
From gloomy care and sorrow free
I'd ever keep my Mary.

MARY.

(AIR: THE DAWTIE OR DARLING).

THERE lives a young lassie
  Far down yon long glen,
How I lo'e that lassie
  There's nae ane can ken!
Oh! a saint's faith may vary,
  But faithfu' I'll be
For weel I lo'e Mary,
  An' Mary lo'es me.

Red, red as the rowan
  Her smiling wee mou'
And white as the gowan
  Her breast and her brow;
We' the foot o' a fairy
  She links o'er the lea—
Oh! weel I lo'e Mary
  And Mary lo'es me.

Where yon tall forest timmer,
  An' lowly broom bower,
To the sunshine o' simmer,
  Spread verdure an' flower;
There, when night clouds the cary,
  Beside her I'll be—
For weel I lo'e Mary
  An' Mary lo'es me!

LOVELY MARY.

(MISS MARY DOUGLASS, OF ALLVA, SCOTLAND).

I'VE seen the lily of the wold,
   I've seen the opening marigold,
Where fairest hues at morn unfold,
     But fairer is my Mary.
How sweet the fringe of mountain burn,
With opening flowers at Spring's return!
How sweet the scent of flow'ry thorn!
     But sweeter is my Mary.

Her heart is gentle, warm and kind;
Her form's not fairer than her mind;
Two sister beauties rarely joined,
     But both in lovely Mary.
As music from the distant steep,
As starlight on the silent deep,
So are my passions lulled asleep
     By love for bonnie Mary.

THE BONNIE BLINK O' MARY'S E'E.

NOW bank and brae are clad in green,
    And scatter'd cowslips sweetly spring;
By Girvan's fairy-haunted stream,
    The birdies flit on wanton wing;
By Cassillis' banks when e'eing fa's,
    There let my Mary meet ur' me,
There catch her ilka glance o' love
    The bonnie blink o' Mary's e'e!

The chiel' who boasts o' world's wealth
    Is often laird o' mickle care;
But Mary she is a' my ain,
    An' Fortune canna gie me mair.
Then let me stray by Cassillis' banks
    Wi' her, the lassie dear to me,
And catch her ilka glance o' love
    The bonnie blink o' Mary's e'e.

MARY AND ME ON THE BRAES O' BEDLAY.

(AIR: HILLS O' GLENOSCHY).

WHEN I think on the sweet smiles o' my lassie,
  My cares flee away like a thief frae the day;
My heart loups light, and I join in a sang,
  Among the sweet birds on the braes o' Bedlay.
How sweet the embrace, yet how honest the wishes,
When luve fa's a-wooin', and modestly blushes,
Whaur Mary an' I meet amang the green bushes,
  That screen us so weel on the braes o' Bedlay.

There's nane sae trig or sae fair as my lassie,
  An' mony a wooer she answers wi' " Nay,"
Wha fain wad ha'e her to lea' me alane,
  An' meet me nae mair on the braes o' Bedlay.
I fear na, I care na, their braggin' o' siller,
Nor a' the fine things they can think on to tell her,
Nae vauntin' can buy her, nae threatnin' can sell her,
  It's luve leads her out to the braes o' Bedlay.

We'll gang by the links o' the wild rowin' burnie,
  Whaur aft in my mornin' o' life I did stray,
Whaur luve was invited and cares were beguiled
  By Mary and me on the braes o' Bedlay.

Sae luvin, sae movin, I'll tell her my story,
Unmixed wi' the deeds o' ambition or glory,
Whaur wide-spreading hawthorns sae ancient and hoary
   Enrich the sweet breeze on the braes o' Bedlay.

WINSOME MARY GRIEVE, OR THE WELLS O' WEARIE.

(AIR: BONNIE HOUSE O' AIRLIE).

SWEETLY shines the sun, on auld Edinbro' town,
   And mak's her look young and cheerie;
Yet I maun awa' to spend the afternoon
   At the lonesome Wells o' Wearie.

And you maun gang wi' me, my winsome Mary Grieve,
   There's naught in the world to fear ye;
For I ha'e asked your mither, an' she has gi'en ye leave
   To gang to the Wells o' Wearie.

Oh, the sun winna blink in thy bonnie blue een,
   Nor tinge the white brow o' my dearie;
For I'll shade a bower wi' rushes lang and green,
   By the lanesome Wells o' Wearie.

But Mary, my luve, beware ye dinna glower,
   At your form, in the water so clearly;
Or the Fairy will change you into a wee, wee flower.
And you'll grow by the Wells o' Wearie!

Yestreen as I wander'd there a' alane,
   I felt unco douf and drearie,
For wanting my Mary a' aroun' me was but pain,
   At the lanesome Wells o' Wearie.

Let fortune or fame, their minions deceive,
   Let fate look gruesome and eerie;
True glory and wealth are mine wi' Mary Grieve,
   When we meet by the Wells o' Wearie.

Then gang wi' me, my bonnie Mary Grieve,
   No danger will daur to come near ye;
For I ha'e asked your mither and she has gi'en ye leave,
   To gang to the Wells o' Wearie!

MARY AND THE FARIES.

" AND where have you been, my Mary,
And where have you been from me?"
"I've been to the top of the Caldon-Low,
The Midsummer night to see."

"And what did you see my Mary,
All up on the Caldon-Low?"
"I saw the blithe sunshine come down,
And I saw the merry winds blow."

"And what did you hear my Mary,
All up on the Caldon-Hill?"
"I heard the drops of the water made,
And the green corn ears to fill."

"Oh tell me all my Mary—
All, all that ever you know:
For you must have seen the faries,
Last night on the Caldon-Low."

"Then listen close to me mother,
Yes, listen mother of mine:
A hundred faries danced last night,
And the Harpers,—they were nine.

And merry was the glee of the harp-strings,
   And their dancing feet so small:
But oh! the sound of their talking was—
   Was merrier far than all.''

" And what were the words my Mary,
   That you did hear them say ? "
" I'll tell you all my mother—
   But let me have my way.

And some they played with the water,
   And rolled it down the hill:
And this they said shall speedily turn
   The poor old miller's mill.

For there has been no water
   Ever since the first of May:
And a busy man shall the miller be
   By the dawning of the day.

Oh! the miller, how he will laugh,
   When he sees the mill-dam rise.
The jolly old miller, how he will laugh,
   Till the tears fill both his eyes.''

And some they seized the little winds,
   That sounded over the hill,
And each put a horn into his mouth,
   And blew so sharp and shrill;—

" And there," said they, " the merry winds go,
 Away from every horn:
And those shall clear the mildew dank,
 From the blind old widow's corn."

And some they brought the brown lintseed,
 And flung it down from the Low—
" And this," said they, " by the sunrise,
 In the weaver's croft shall grow."

   *   *   *   *   *   *

And then up spoke a merry Brownie,
 With a long beard on his chin—
" I have spun up all the tow," said he,
 And I want some more to spin.

I've spun a piece of hempen cloth,—
 And I want to spin another;
A fair fine sheet for Mary's bed,
 And an apron for her mother."

And with that I could not help but laugh,
 And I laughed out loud and free,
And then on the top of the Caldon-Low
 There was no one left but me!

And all on the top of the Caldon-Low,
 The mists were cold and gray,
And nothing I saw but the mossy stones
 That round about me lay.

But as I came down from the hill-top,
    I heard afar below,
How busy the jolly miller was,
    And how merry the wheel did go.

And I peeped into the widow's field,
    And sure enough was seen,
The yellow'd ears of the mildewed corn
    All standing stiff and green.

And down by the weaver's croft I stole,
    To see if the flax were high:
And I saw the weaver at his gate
    With the good news in his eye.

Now this is all I heard mother,
    And all that I did see,
So, prithee, make my bed mother,
    For I'm tired as I can be!"

                MARY HOWITT.

MARY, "THE LASS O' ISLA."

HE: "AH, Mary sweetest maid farewell!
      My hopes are flown for a's to wreck,
Heaven guard you love, and heal your heart,
    Though mine, alas! maun break."

SHE: "Dearest lad, what ills betide?
     Is Willie to his love untrue?
Engaged the morn to be his bride,
    An' ha'e ye, ha'e ye ta'en the rue?"

HE: "Ye canna wear a ragged gown,
     Or beggar wed ur' naught ava;
My kye are drown'd, my house is down
    My last sheep lies aneath the snaw."

SHE: "Tell na me o' storm or flood,
     Or sheep a' smoor'd ayont the hill;
For Willie's sake I Willie lo'ed,
    Though poor, ye are my Willie still."

HE: "Ye canna thole the wind and rain,
     Or wander friendless far fra hame;
Cheer, cheer your heart; some other swain
    Will soon blot out lost Willie's name."

SHE: " I'll tak my bundle in my hand
       And wipe the dew-drop frae my e'e;
    I'll wander wi' ye o'er the land
       I'll venture wi' ye o'er the sea."

   *   *   *   *   *   *

HE: " Forgi'e me, 'twas all a snare;
       My flocks are safe, we needna' part;
    I'd forfeit them, and ten times mair
       To clasp thee Mary to my heart."

SHE: " How could ye wi' my feelings sport
       Or doubt a heart sae warm and true?
    I maist could wish ye mischief for 't,
       But canna wish aught ill to you."

ADIEU, ADIEU FOR AYE MARY.

(OR "THE BRAES OF AUCHINBLAE").

AS clear is Luther's wave I ween,
    As gay the grove, the vale as green;
But, oh! the days that we have seen
       Are fled, and fled for aye, Mary!

Oh! we have often fondly stray'd
In Fordoun's green embow'ring glade
And marked the moonbeam as it played
       On Luther's bonnie wave, Mary!

Since then full many a year and day
With me have slowly pass'd away,
Far from the braes of Auchinblae
   And far from love and thee Mary!

And we must part again, my dear,
It is not mine to linger here;
Yes, we must part—and oh! I fear,
   We meet not here again Mary!

For on Cullodin's bloody field,
Our hapless prince's fate is seal'd—
Last night to me it was reveal'd
   Sooth as the word of Heaven, Mary!

And 'ere tomorrow's sun shall shine
Upon the heights of Galloguhine,
A thousand victims at the shrine
   Of tyranny, shall bleed, Mary!

Hark! Hark! they come—the foemen come—
I go, but wheresoe'r I roam,
With thee my heart remains at home.
   Adieu! adieu, for aye, Mary!

MARY STEEL.

I'LL think o' thee, my Mary Steel,
 When the lark begins to sing,
And a thousan', thousan' joyfu' hearts
 Are welcoming the spring;
When the merle and the blackbird build their nest
 In the bushy forest tree,
And a' things under the sky seem blest
 My thoughts shall be o' thee.

I'll think o' thee my Mary Steel,
 When the simmer spreads her flowers,
And the lilly blooms, and the ivy twines
 In beauty round the bowers;
When the cushat coos in the leafy wood,
 And the lambs sport o'er the lea,
And every heart's in its happiest mood,
 My thoughts shall be o' thee.

I'll think o' thee, my Mary Steel
 When harv'st blythe days begin,
And shearers ply in the yellow ripe field
 The foremost rig to win;
When the shepherd brings his ewes to the fauld,
 Where light-hair'd lassies be,
And mony a tale o' love is tauld,
 My thoughts shall be o' thee.

I'll think o' thee, my Mary Steel,
  When the winds rave high,
And the tempest wild is pourin' down,
  Frae the dark and troubled sky;
When a hopeless wail is heard on land,
  And shrieks frae the roaring sea,
And the wreck o' Nature seems at hand
  My thoughts shall be o' thee!

THOU KEN'ST MARY HAY.

(THE AULD HUSBAND'S APPEAL TO HIS MARY).

TUNE: "BONNIE MARY HAY."

THOU ken'st Mary Hay, that I loe thee weel,
  My ain auld wife sae canty and leal,
Then what gars thee stand wi' the tear in thine e'e,
And look aye sae wae, when thou look'st at me?

Dost thou miss Mary Hay, the soft bloom o' my cheek,
And the hair curling round it sae gentie and sleek?
For the snaw's on my head, and the roses are gane,
Since that day o' days I first ca'd thee my ain.

But though, Mary Hay, my auld e'en be grown dim,
An' age wi' its frost, mak's cauld every limb,
My heart thou kens weel has nae cauldness for thee
For summer returns at the blink o' thine e'e.

The miser hands firmer and firmer his gold
The ivy sticks close to the tree when it's old,
And still thou grow'st dearer to me, Mary Hay
As a' else turns eerie, and life wears away.

We maun part, Mary Hay, when our journey is done,
But I'll meet thee again in the bright world aboon,
Then what gars thee stand wi' the tear in thine e'e,
And look aye sae wae, when thon look'st at me?

MARY OF SWEET ABERFOYLE.

THE sun had na peeped frae behind the dark billow,
   The slow-sinking moon half illumin'd the scene,
As I lifted my head frae my care-haunted pillow,
   And waner'd to muse on the days that were gane.
Sweet hope seem'd to smile o'er ideas romantic,
   An' gay were the dreams that my soul would beguile;
But my eyes fill'd wi' tears as I view'd the Atlantic,
   An' thought on my Mary of sweet Aberfoyle.

Though frae from my home in a tropical wild-wood,
   Yet the fields o' my forefathers rose on my view;
And I wept when I thought on the days of my childhood,
   An' the vision more painful the brighter it grew.

Sweet days! when my bosom with rapture was swelling,
　Though I knew it not then, it was love made me smile;
Oh! the snaw-wreath is pure where the moonbeams are
　　dwelling,
　Yet as pure is my Mary of sweet Aberfoyle.

　　*　　*　　*　　*　　*　　*

When the mirk cloud o' fortune aboon my head gathers,
　An' the golden show'r fa's where it ne'er fell before,
Ah! then I'll revisit the land of my father's,
　And clasp to this bosom the lass I adore.
Hear me ye angels, who watch o'er my maiden,
　(Like ane o' yoursel's she is free frae a' guile),
Pure as was love in the garden of Eden,
　Sae pure is my Mary of sweet Aberfoyle.

MARIE.

(SINGING).

FROM THE FRENCH OF ALFRED DE MUSSET.

THE beaut'ous flower of spring
　　Opens its leaves in the wood, and
Smiles,—a curious mys'try fine,
Stirred by the zephyr's mood,
And its stalk so light and fresh
Feels its petals slowly open;—
Down to its roots in the earth,
Tremb'ling with joyful emotion.

'Tis thus when my gentle Marie
While singing, her dear lips part;
Raising above her azure eyes,
Her sensitive soul and heart—
Seems bathed in a buoyant fire
Of harmony and of light,
Then rising in tremulous joy
Aspires to the Heaven's so bright.

TRANS. E. V. B.

A FRENCH SAILOR'S ADIEU TO MARIE.

A FLOWER FOR RESPONSE.

"OUR ship is about to sail Marie; for long I shall not see
thee,
In going so far away may I have a keepsake?
If not for love at least for hope: I'm going, adieu Marie!
I leave to-morrow.
If you will regret me, oh! I beg—
Give me that flower darling your hand has touched.

If that flower were given to me, by you,
Even in leaving, I should feel some joy;
And when far away from you, that faded rose,
Will be ever there, ever there on my heart."

The poor child trembled 'neath his gaze;
Sad and dreaming she implored God's help, and he, in a
voice

Both tender and reproachful, said:
" You're silent, ah! you do not love me—I'm going
My heart is wounded.   Adieu! I go to-morrow."
He was turning away, when that cherished flower
Dropped from her hand into his.

FROM "MUSIC OF THE WATERS," BY L. A. SMITH.

TO MARY QUEEN OF SCOTS.

(ON HER DEPARTURE FROM FRANCE).

FROM THE FRENCH.

"THE day that was to bear her far away!
       Why was I mortal to behold that day?
O! France, where are thy ancient champions gone,
Roland, Rinaldo? is there living none
Her steps to follow, and her safety guard,
And deem her lovely looks their best reward!

      *   *   *   *   *

All beauty granted as a boon to earth,
That is, has been, or ever can have birth,
Compar'd to her's is void, and Nature's care,
Ne'er form'd a creature so divinely fair.

      *   *   *   *   *

Wherever Destiny her path may lead
Fresh springing flow'rs will bloom beneath her tread,
All Nature will rejoice, the waves be bright,
The tempest check its fury at her sight;
The sea be calm; her beauty to behold,
The Sun shall crown her with its rays of gold—
Unless he fears, should he approach her throne
Her Majesty should quite eclipse his own! "

PIERRE DE RONSARD.

AN ALLEGORY ON MARY QUEEN OF SCOTS.

(FROM THE FRENCH).

THERE'S a bonnie wild rose on the mountain side,
  In the glare of noon it hath drooped and died:
Soft and still is the evening shower,
Pattering kindly on brake and bower,
But it falls too late on the perished flower.

There's a lamb lies lost at the head of the glen,
Lost and missed from shieling and pen;
The shepherd has sought it in toil and heat;
And sore he strove when he heard it bleat,
Ere he wins to the lamb, it lies dead at his feet.

The mist is gathering ghostly and chill,
And the weary maid cometh down from the hill,

The weary maid—but she's down at last;
And she tried the door, but the door is fast;
For the sun is down, and the Curfew past.

Too late for the Rose the evening rain;
Too late the lamb for the Shepherd's pain;
Too late at her home the maiden's stroke;
Too late for the Plea when the doom hath been spoke;
Too late the Balm when the heart is broke!

PIERRE DE CHASTELARD.

ADIEU DE MARIE STUART.

(FROM THE FRENCH OF BÉRANGER).

" A DIEU beloved France, adieu,
    Thou ever will be dear to me,
Land which my happy childhood knew
    I feel I die, in quitting thee.

*   *   *   *   *   *

When on my brow the lillies bright,
    Before admiring throngs I wore,
'Twas not my state that charm'd their sight,
    They loved my youthful beauty more.
Although the Scot with sombre mien,
    Gives me a crown, I still repine,
I only wish'd to be a queen,
    Ye sons of France, to call you mine.

Adieu beloved France, &c.

Love, glory, genius crowded round,
   My youthful spirit to elate;
On Caledonia's rugged ground,
   Ah! changed indeed will be my fate.
E'en now terrific omens seem
   To threaten ill—my heart is scared;
I see, as in a hideous dream
   A scaffold for my death prepared.

     Adieu beloved France, &c.

France, from amid the countless fears,
   The Stuart's hapless child may feel,
E'en as she now looks through her tears,
   So will her glances seek thee still.
Alas! the ship too swiftly sails,
   O'er me are spreading other skies,
And night with humid mantle veils
   Thy fading coast from these sad eyes.

     Adieu beloved France, &c.

VERSES FOR THE FÊTE OF MARY.

(FROM "LE POÈTE DE COEUR."—BÉRANGER).

WHAT? to thee Mary tune a song again?
  No, no in truth I may not dare obey,
Nerved is my muse to try a loftier strain,
  And t'wards the Court, at length she wings her way.

     *   *   *   *   *   *

All patriotic notions now are hiss'd;
  To reckon readily's the only thing,
An ode I'm writing to an egotist
  Mary for thee no longer can I sing

          They're buying pipe and lyre
            'Tis then full time for me
          Like others to aspire
            Court Lauriat to be!

Thy doubts, dear Mary, tell me whence they came
  That thus to change, should be thy lover's lot?
Country and honor, liberty and fame,
  Are merely words—and men discount them not.
To offer flattery to the great I'm learning
  And songs for thee—on them might satire fling;
No, no, where'er my heart might fain be turning
  Mary, for thee no longer can I sing
          They're buying pipe and lyre, &c.

MARIE'S DREAM.

(FROM THE FRENCH OF G. LEMOINE).

" AND you would quit Marie,
   Your mother dear,
And Paris you would see,
   While she weeps here?
Yet stay awhile, oh! stay,
   You need not go till morning breaks,
Sleep here until the day;
   'Tis better, poor Marie,
To pause as yet;
   For all at Paris they tell me,
Their God forget.
   Perchance you may, my poor Marie,
Your mother and your God forget."

*   *   *   *   *   *

She leaves her native home
   With weeping eyes,
To Paris she has come—
   Oh bright surprise!
There all appears to trace,
   In lines of gold her future lot;
And dazzling dreams efface
   The image of her humble cot.

Heaven, when two years have past
　　Bids her return,
To her old home at last—
　　She comes to mourn.
" Sister! oh happy day—
　　My brother too I see!
And where's my mother pray ? "
　　" She died through losing thee."

At once the vision fled—
　　She sleeps no more.
The watchful mother at her bed
　　Sits as before:
Marie cries out, " No Paris now for me"
　　(Her eyes with tears of joy are wet),
" For then perhaps, your poor Marie
　　Her God and mother might forget!"

AN AVOWAL.

(FROM THE FRENCH OF BARALLI).

OH, do not refuse me, I love thee Marie,
    Than life thou'rt a hundred times dearer to me;
  My worship is such as we raise to the skies,
I love thy clear voice, and thy brow ever fair,
Thy modest attire, and thy light sunny hair,
  O Marie! and the blue of thine eyes.

Oh give me that love, undivided—the whole,
Which wakens with life, and expires with the soul;
    That true woman's love, and in turn I'll adore;
And when passing years write their trace on thy brow,
Those moments of joy which enrapture us now
  Marie, to thy heart I'll restore.

But if thou'lt not love me, still let me, I pray
Adore thy blue eye, and its pure gentle ray;
    Those features which never can fade from the sight;
And let me thy sweet eighteen summers combine
In one flow'ry wreath, and thy forehead entwine
  O Marie! with love and delight.

MARIE'S LOVER.

(LE PRISONNIÈRE EN GUERRE, BY BÉRANGER).

"MARIE, 'tis late put by thy work
 The Shepherd's star has risen!"
"Nay, mother, nay, our village lad
 Pines in a foreign prison;
Far off from home, on distant sea
He yielded—but the last was he."

  "Spin, spin, dear Marie, spin
   To send the prisoner aid;
  Spin, spin, dear Marie spin
   For him who's captive made."

 "Well if thou wilt the lamp I'll light
 But child, thy tears still flow!"
"Mother, he frets himself to death
 The Briton mocks his woe.
How Adrian loved me when a boy
With him about our hearth, what joy!"

  Spin, dear Marie, spin, &c.

 "Ah were I not myself too old
 I'd spin child for his sake."
O! mother send to him I love,
 All, all that I can make;

Rose bids me to her wedding go—
Hark! there's the fiddler!   No, no, no!''

    Spin, dear Marie, spin, &c.

*   *   *   *   *   *

'' Daughter that he thy husband was
    I dream'd again last night;
And always ere the month be out
    These dreams of mine come right!''

    Spin, spin, dear Marie spin
      To send the prisoner aid;
    Spin, spin, dear Marie, spin,
      For him who's captive made.''

MARY STUART IN FOTHERINGAY PARK.

(FROM THE GERMAN OF FRED. SCHILLER'S TRAGEDY,
MARY STUART).

O LET me enjoy my new freedom,
    Let me as a child on the green carpet
Of the meadow, go forward as on wings.
Descended have I from my gloomy prison;
Holds me no more the sorrowful cell,
Let me to the full assuage my thirst,
My famishing thirst for the free air!

  ✻ ✻ ✻ ✻ ✻

Thanks, thanks, for these friendly green trees
That shut out the sight of my prison walls!
I will here dream that I am free and happy;
Why waken me from my sweetest vision?
Surrounds me not the wide expanse of Heaven?
The aspect is free and chainless—
Spreading in measureless distance out.
Yonder where rise the misty green hills
Begins the bounds of my kingdom,
And those clouds which since mid day
Chase joyfully each other in their course
Seek, over the distant ocean, the coast of France.

Hasten ye clouds! Sailors of the air!
Who with you journeys—who ship your way,
Salute for me my youth's fair land.
I, a prisoner and in bonds;
Alas! I have no other ambassador!
Free in the air is your triumphant way,
 You are not subjects of this English Queen.

      Trans. E. V. B.

MORTIMER'S INTERVIEW WITH MARIA STUART.

(FROM THE GERMAN OF SCHILLER'S TRAGEDY "MARIA STUART").

"ONE day,
　　As I looked about me in the Bishop's house
A woman's picture met my startled eye;
Of wonderful and sympathetic charm it was:
How powerfully it moved me in my deepest soul!
Unable to control my feelings, helpless stood I there.
Then said to me the Bishop, "Well may
You stand impressed before this picture,
Not only represents it, the most beautiful woman that lives,
But she is also the one who deserves the sincerest pity:
For our faith she is a resigned sufferer,
And 'tis in your father-land where she suffers."

　　*　　*　　*　　*　　*　　*

"Now see I Queen, your very self!
Not your mere picture! O what a treasure holds
This castle! It is no jail! Rather a Hall of the Gods
More brilliant than the Sovereign Court
Of England. O! what happiness is granted
Those who breathe this air with you!
Well have they right, you so deeply to conceal!
All England's youth would rise,

No sword lie idle in its scabbard
And the revolt, with head of giant
Would—through this peaceful island stride
Saw but the Briton once, his rightful Queen!"

TRANS. E. V. B.

O MARY QUEEN OF MERCY.

(FROM THE GERMAN OF KARL SIMROCK).

THERE lived a Knight long years ago,
    Proud, carnal, vain, devotionless,
Of God above, or Hell below,
    He took no thought, but undismayed,
Pursued his course of wickedness.
    His heart was rock; he never prayed
To be forgiven for all his treasons;
He only said, at certain seasons,
    "O *Mary*, Queen of Mercy!"

Years rolled, and found him still the same
Still draining Pleasure's poison-bowl;
    Yet felt he now and then some shame;
    The torment of the Undying Worm
At whiles woke in his trembling soul;
    And then, though powerless to reform
Would he, in hope to appease that sternest
Avenger, cry, and more in earnest,
    "O *Mary*, Queen of Mercy!"

At last youth's riotous time was gone,
And loathing now came after sin.
　With locks yet brown he felt as one
　　Grown grey at heart; and oft, with tears,
He tried, but all in vain, to win
　　From the dark desert of his years
　One flower of hope; yet morn and e'ening,
　He still cried, but with deeper meaning,
　　"O *Mary*, Queen of Mercy!"

A happier mind, a holier mood,
A purer spirit, ruled him now;
　No more in thrall to flesh and blood,
　　He took a pilgrim-staff in hand,
And under a religious vow,
　　Travalled his way to Pommerland,
　There entered he an humble cloister,
　Exclaiming, while his eyes grew moister,
　　"O *Mary*, Queen of Mercy!"

Here, shorn and cowled, he laid his cares
Aside, and wrought for God alone.
　Albeit he sang no choral prayers,
　　Nor matin hymn nor laud could learn,
He mortified his flesh to stone;
　　For him no penance was too stern;
　And often prayed he on his lonely
　Cell-couch at night, but still said only,
　　"O *Mary*, Queen of Mercy!"

And thus he lived long, long; and, when
God's angels called him, thus he died.
   Confession made he none to man,
     Yet, when they anointed him with oil,
He seemed already glorified.
     His penances, his tears, his toil,
Were past; and now, with passionate sighing
Praise thus broke from his lips while dying,
     " O *Mary*, Queen of Mercy!"

   They burried him with mass and song
Aneath a little knoll so green;
     But lo a wondrous sight!—ere long
       Rose blooming, from that verdant mound,
The fairest lilly ever seen;
     And on its petal edges round,
Relieving their translucent whiteness.
Did shine these words in gold-hued brightness,
     " O *Mary*, Queen of Mercy!"

   And would God's angels give thee power,
Thou, dearest reader, mightst behold
     The fibres of this holy flower
       Upspringing from the dead man's heart,
In tremulous threads of white and gold;
     Then wouldst thou choose the better part!
And thenceforth flee Sin's foul suggestions;
Thy sole response to mocking questions
     " O *Mary*, Queen of Mercy!"
               TRANS. BY J. C. MANGIN.

MARIA'S ASCENSION.

FROM THE SPANISH.

L ADY, thou mountest slowly
O'er the bright cloud, while music sweetly plays;
Blest, who thy mantle holy
With outstretched hand may seize,
And rise with thee to the Infinite of Days.

* * * * * *

Around, behind, before thee
Bright angels wait, that watched thee from thy birth,
A crown of stars is o'er thee,
The pale moon of the earth—
Thou supernatural Queen, nearest in light and worth.

LUIS PONCE DE LEON.

SPANISH BALLAD.

O MARY would'st thou but believe,
    A heart that knows not to deceive,
  Alas! no longer free:
That faithful heart would truly tell
The secret charm, the tender spell
  That bound it first to thee.
'Tis not, that cradled in thine eyes
The wily Cupid ever lies
  On couches dipped in dew.
'Tis not because those eyes have won,
Their temper'd light from April sun,
  From Heaven their tints of blue.
No, dearest, no, but from my soul
It was a little smile that stole
  The cherish'd sweets of rest;
And ever since, from morn till night.
That little smile, still haunts my sight,
  In dimples gaily drest.
O! Mary would'st thou but believe
A heart that knows not to decieve
  You'd quickly set it free;
For liberty within thy arms
Is Paradise in all its charms
    'Tis Heaven alone with thee.

STEVEN'S TRANS.

FAIR MARY.

(FROM THE SPANISH.)

TELL me thou ancient mariner
  That sailest on the sea,
If ship, or sail, or Evening Star
  Be half so fair as she?

Tell me thou gallant cavalier,
  Whose shining arms I see,
If steed, or sword or battle field
  Can charm thy soul as she?

Tell me thou noble hunter
  O'er rock and hill and lea
If stately buck or gentle doe
  Be half so fair as she?

'TIS MARY LEADS MY THOUGHTS ASTRAY.

(FROM THE SPANISH).

"NAY! Shepherd, nay! thou art unwary—
    Thy flocks are wandering far away."
"Alas! I know it well—'tis Mary
Who leads my troubled thoughts astray."

" Look, Shepherd! look—how far they rove!
Why so forgetful? call them yet."
    " O! he who is forgot by love,
    Will soon, too soon, all else forget."
" Come leave those thoughts so dark and dreary,
And with your browsing flocks be gay."
    "Alas, no! 'tis vain, 'tis vain,—Mary
Leads all my troubled thoughts astray."

" 'Tis love then, Shepherd! O, depart,
And drive away the cheating boy."
    "Alas! he's seated in my heart,
    And rules it with tumultuous joy."
" Nay! Shepherd, wake thee, dare not tarry,
For thou art in a thorny way."
    "Ah, no! 'tis vain, 'tis vain,—for Mary
Leads all my troubled thoughts astray."

"Throw off this yoke, young Shepherd, be
Joyous and mirthsome as before."
   "O what are mirth and joy to me?
   They on my woes no joy can pour."
"Thou did'st refuse to dance, did'st tarry,
When laughing maidens were at play."
   "I know I did—alas 'tis Mary
   That leads my troubled thoughts astray."

"Then tell thy love—perchance 'tis hid—
And send a missive scribbled o'er."—
   "Alas! my friend—I did, I did,—
   Which, ere the maid had read, she tore."
"Then hang the maid—the foul fiend carry
A pestilence through all her flocks."
   "O no, forbear!—nor threaten Mary
   With sorrow's frowns, nor misery's shocks."

"BY HER NAME I HAVE CALLED THEE."*

(FROM THE ITALIAN OF GINTIO CARCANS).

SLEEP, sleep, sleep! my little girl,
   Mother is near thee: Sleep, unfurl,
Thy veil o'er the cradle where baby lies!
Dream baby, of angels in the skies!

* The name of the Madonna—Mary.

On the sorrowful earth in hopeless quest
Passes the exile without rest.
Wherever he goes in sun or snow
Trouble and pain beside him go,
> But when I look upon thy sleep,
> And hear thy breathing soft and deep,
> My soul turns with a faith serene
> To days of sorrow that have been;
> And I feel that of love and happiness
> Heaven has given my life excess:
> The Lord in His mercy gave me thee
> And thou in truth art part of me.

Thou know'st not as I bend above thee
How much I love thee, how much I love thee;
Thou art the very life of my heart,
Thou art my joy, my life, my smart!
Thy day begins uncertain, child,
Thou art a blossom in the wild,
But over thee with his wings abroad,
Blossom, watches the angel of God.

> *   *   *   *   *   *

> And over thee my own delight,
> Watches that Sweet Mother day and night,
> To whom the exiles consecrate
> Alter and heart in every fate.
> By HER name, I have called my little girl,
> But on life's sea in the tempest's whirl
> Thy hapless father, my darling, may,
> Only tremble, and only pray.

NATIONAL RUSSIAN SONG TO MARY.

(TRANSLATED BY SIR JOHN BOWRING, F. L. S).

NOISY nightingale! be still,
    Hear'st thou not the sweeter thrill
        Of my Mary,
        Of my Fairy,
From the cottage? through the trees
Born on breath of western breeze?

As the skylark from her height,
Midst the dews of opening light
        Sweetly singeth,
        Joy upspringeth
From the heart that song to hear
So I love thy voice, my dear.

Turn I towards the window-seat—
Give me one soft glance my sweet!
        Kind is Mary,
        Kind my fairy,
Joyous as a summer's day
In the mildest smile of May.

Then her heart its folds unveils,
And she sings its secret tales:
        Gently flowing,
        Mildly glowing,

O how sweetly falls the strain!
O how fascinating then!

When upon the harpsicord,
Music leads the mournful word
    And the spirit
    Sighs to hear it,
Led by her in willing chain—
Who was ever like her then?

Who? Two Marys can not be,
Mary! life's sweet witchery!
    Mary! bless me,
    And caress me;
Kings might envy, for thou art,
Mary! thou, my heart of heart.

Peace! she sighs—thou window fly
Open; let me drink her sigh,
    Glowing, blushing,
    Thither rushing
Could I steal one rapturous kiss—
Sing sweet bird! thy song of bliss.

MARY'S EYES—OR THE FORTUNE TELLER.

(FROM THE MODERN GREEK BY GEORGE DROSINÊS).

" NOW tell me aged Sorceress, who dost all fortunes know,
What good, what ill-fate shall be mine, as through
the world I go?"
" My boy ere thou of twenty years shalt be a stripling brave,
Thou for a little nut-brown maid, and for her charms shall
rave:
The blooming springtide of thy youth to her shall fully give,
But she, shall all thy passion's glow, with this alone repay,
That she shall steal the happiness of thy whole life away."

" The first came true indeed, and thee, little one I adore,
But for the old wife's other words, I ne'er will trust them
more,
Since unto me of love and joy give surer prophecies—
Other dark sorceresses twain—they, Mary, are thine eyes."

TRANS. BY F. M. McPHERSON.

MARY WASHINGTON.

O'ER this bright galexy of Marys fair,
   One towers above them all, beyond compare,
A patriot soul—great in herself,
   And greater in her son,
   Need we to name her?—WASHINGTON.

E. V. B.

HOMAGE TO MARY WASHINGTON.

This is a first incompleted draught of the long poem written by
Mrs. Lydia H. Sigourney on the occasion of the laying of the
corner-stone of the Monument to the mother of President George
Washington, at Fredericksburg, by President Jackson, May, 7, 1833.

"WE come
   To do thee homage, Mother of our chief.
Fit honor—such as honoreth him who pays:—
Methinks we see thee as in olden time,
Simple in garb, majestic and serene,
Unmoved by pomp and circumstance; in truth
Inflexible, and with a Spartan zeal.
*   *   *   For the might that clothed
The 'Pater Patriae,' for the glorious deeds

That make Mount Vernon's tomb a Mecca shrine
To all the earth, these to thee are due.
                    Rise sculptured pile!
And show a race unborn WHO rests below
And earned a monument,
Should rise above the stars!''

www.ingramcontent.com/pod-product-compliance
Lightning Source LLC
Chambersburg PA
CBHW021136020726
47500CB00003B/1107